DEVELOPMENT CENTRE STUDIES

CHINA'S LONG MARCH TO AN OPEN ECONOMY

by
Kiichiro Fukasaku and David Wall,
with Mingyuan Wu

DEVELOPMENT CENTRE
OF THE ORGANISATION FOR ECONOMIC CO-OPERATION AND DEVELOPMENT

ORGANISATION FOR ECONOMIC CO-OPERATION AND DEVELOPMENT

Pursuant to Article 1 of the Convention signed in Paris on 14th December 1960, and which came into force on 30th September 1961, the Organisation for Economic Co-operation and Development (OECD) shall promote policies designed:

— to achieve the highest sustainable economic growth and employment and a rising standard of living in Member countries, while maintaining financial stability, and thus to contribute to the development of the world economy;

— to contribute to sound economic expansion in Member as well as non-member countries in the process of economic development; and

— to contribute to the expansion of world trade on a multilateral, non-discriminatory basis in accordance with international obligations.

The original Member countries of the OECD are Austria, Belgium, Canada, Denmark, France, Germany, Greece, Iceland, Ireland, Italy, Luxembourg, the Netherlands, Norway, Portugal, Spain, Sweden, Switzerland, Turkey, the United Kingdom and the United States. The following countries became Members subsequently through accession at the dates indicated hereafter: Japan (28th April 1964), Finland (28th January 1969), Australia (7th June 1971), New Zealand (29th May 1973) and Mexico (18th May 1994). The Commission of the European Communities takes part in the work of the OECD (Article 13 of the OECD Convention).

The Development Centre of the Organisation for Economic Co-operation and Development was established by decision of the OECD Council on 23rd October 1962 and comprises twenty-two Member countries of the OECD: Austria, Belgium, Canada, Denmark, Finland, France, Germany, Greece, Iceland, Ireland, Italy, Japan, Luxembourg, Mexico, the Netherlands, Norway, Portugal, the United Kingdom, the United States, Spain, Sweden and Switzerland, as well as the Republic of Korea since April 1992 and Argentina and Brazil from March 1994.

The purpose of the Centre is to bring together the knowledge and experience available in Member countries of both economic development and the formulation and execution of general economic policies; to adapt such knowledge and experience to the actual needs of countries or regions in the process of development and to put the results at the disposal of the countries by appropriate means.

The Centre has a special and autonomous position within the OECD which enables it to enjoy scientific independence in the execution of its task. Nevertheless, the Centre can draw upon the experience and knowledge available in the OECD in the development field.

Publié en français sous le titre :
LA «LONGUE MARCHE» DE LA CHINE VERS UNE ÉCONOMIE OUVERTE

Foreword

This study was produced as part of the Development Centre's research programme under the theme of "Globalisation and Regionalisation".

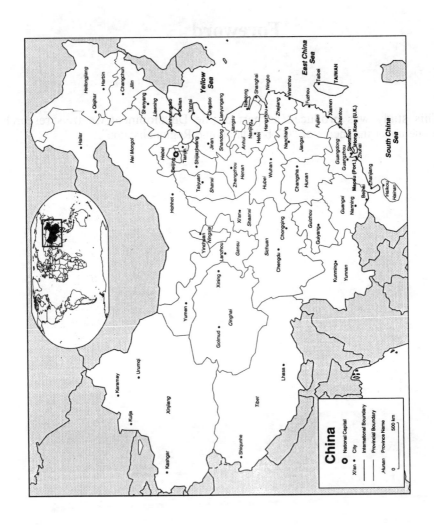

Table of Contents

List of Tables and Figures

Acknowledgements

The study began in spring 1992 as a follow-up to the Development Centre's research project on Globalisation and Regionalisation in Pacific Asia. A grant from the Government of Japan is gratefully acknowledged.

This monograph is the final product of the study and is based on several papers written at various stages over the past two years, including Fukasaku (1992b), Fukasaku and Wu (1993), Wall (1992b), Wall and Fukasaku (1994) and Wu (1993).

We are grateful for helpful comments from Colin Bradford and Charles Oman at an early stage of the study. We are also grateful for research co-operation with Fudan University in Shanghai and the National Centre for Development Studies at Australian National University.

Thanks are extended to Michèle Fleury-Brousse and her staff at the Centre's Statistical Unit for able assistance, and to Colm Foy for useful editorial advice. Special thanks are also extended to Elley Mao, Principal Economist of the Economic Services Branch at the Central Government Office of Hong Kong, as well as the Census and Statistics Department of Hong Kong for providing us with statistical materials.

List of Acronyms

ADP	Automatic Data Processing (Equipment)
ASEAN	Association of South-East Asian Nations
CCP	Chinese Communist Party
CIS	Commonwealth of Independent States
CMS	Constant Market Share
ETDZ	Economic and Technological Development Zones
FDI	Foreign Direct Investment
FTC	Foreign Trade Corporation
ISR	Internal Settlement Rate
MFA	Multifibres Arrangement
MOFTEC	Ministry of Foreign Trade And Economic Co-operation
MOFERT	Ministry of Foreign Economic Relations and Trade
NIE	Newly Industrialized Economy
OEM	Original Equipment Manufacturing
PLA	People's Liberation Army
PPP	Purchasing Power Parity
PRC	People's Republic of China
SEZ	Special Economic Zones
SITC	Standard International Trade Classification

Preface

The aim of the Development Centre's research on Globalisation and Regionalisation was to provide a better understanding of the economic and political forces that are working for — and against — the formation of regional economic groupings in Europe, the Western Hemisphere and Pacific Asia, and how those forces interact with the forces promoting globalisation.

In the 1990s, Pacific Asia has come to play an increasingly important role as an "engine of growth" for the world economy. Its economic dynamism owes much to China's rapid growth, which was made possible by the launching of policy reforms, collectively known as "Reform and Opening Up", in late 1978. As China becomes a major player in world trade and investment, it is important for OECD Member countries to know more about changes in China's trade and investment regimes, particularly at a time when China is making a great effort to rejoin the General Agreement on Tariffs and Trade (GATT).

This study focuses on the evolution of China's "opening-up" policy and its implications both for the regional economies and for the economies of OECD countries. It presents a detailed analysis of what the authors call "open-economy reforms" in China, namely, the reform of foreign trade and exchange regimes, the establishment of a legal and institutional framework for foreign direct investment and the establishment of Special Economic Zones (SEZs) and other development zones. One of the main findings is that as a result of its open-economy reforms, China's exports have increasingly specialised in a relatively narrow range of manufactured products, mainly of the labour-intensive kind, like those of the NIEs. This will increase pressures on other lower-income economies of the region, such as Indonesia and the Philippines, to liberalise further their trade and investment regimes.

The study also examines some of the implications of China's entry into the world market for the policy of OECD Member countries. What would happen to the OECD countries' economies if China's exports were to continue to grow at their current pace? In some OECD countries, especially those in western Europe, where rising unemployment is an acute political and economic issue, there are serious concerns over competitive pressures from China. The study shows, however, that the share of Chinese products in OECD-Europe imports is much smaller than that in Japan, and urges OECD countries to keep their markets open, as this is a necessary condition for China to pursue its ongoing policy reform and maintain its growth momentum, which is crucial for world economic recovery.

Initiatives in 1994 by the Chinese authorities to unify the dual exchange-rate regime and to reform the tax system, which is expected to increase the revenue of the central government, enhance the political credibility of China's economic reform.

In providing a thorough analysis of China's opening-up policy and examining its implications from the perspective of Pacific Asia, the study makes an important contribution to the Development Centre's research on Globalisation and Regionalisation. It is also a significant addition to the Centre's continuing research on China.

Jean Bonvin
President
OECD Development Centre
August 1994

Executive Summary

At the landmark Third Plenary Session of the 11th Central Committee of the Chinese Communist Party (CCP) in December 1978, the People's Republic of China embarked on the reform of its centrally planned economy to an open market economy. The country's macroeconomic performance during the post-reform period is impressive. Gross domestic product (GDP) increased by 10 per cent per year in real terms in the 1980s, though this growth rate declined to 4 per cent in 1989-90 as a result of the implementation of anti-inflationary measures. As it enters the 1990s, China has resumed rapid economic growth, recording double-digit rates since 1992. Fifteen years of "Reform and Opening Up" have brought China to the centre stage of East Asian economic dynamism.

China's reform and growth experiences since late 1978 have been of direct relevance to the reform strategies of other economies in transition in Europe, Asia and elsewhere. Given China's size (with a population of 1.2 billion) and outward orientation, the reform and growth of its economy also have important implications for neighbouring economies in East and Southeast Asia as well as for OECD Member countries, which are China's main trade and investment partners. What lessons, if any, can be drawn from the Chinese experience of economic transition? What are the implications of China's economic transition for the outside world?

This study focuses on the development of China's open-economy reforms since late 1978 and their economic consequences. "Open-economy reforms" refer to the reform of foreign-trade and exchange regimes, the establishment of a legal and institutional framework for foreign direct investment, and the establishment of Special Economic Zones (SEZs) and other development zones. Although experiences with open-economy reforms have been mixed, China has been successful in causing strong supply responses to market incentives created by these reforms, even though they are partial and incomplete. However, a partially reformed economy tends to produce within Chinese society a marked social division between those with privileged access to markets and those without. It is thus imperative for China to continue its "long march" towards the establishment of an open market economy.

China's Transition Strategy

China's gradualist strategy of transition to a market economy is often contrasted with the so-called "big-bang" strategy adopted by Poland, Russia and the former Czechoslovakia. China's transition strategy may perhaps best be described as one of "feeling for the stones while crossing the river".

China's economic reform began without any comprehensive blueprint or timetable. This strategy allowed Chinese reformers to experiment on a limited scale, and when policies proved successful, the government endorsed them. A main feature of China's policy reform has been first to enact politically crucial but not very specific "enabling laws", allowing the government to introduce more specific measures when political and economic conditions are met.

The relative success of policy reform in China compared to that of other economies in transition, particularly in eastern Europe, should *not* be construed as confirming the view that the gradual approach is the best. Differences in initial conditions — internal and external — between economies in transition are so large and important that any generalisation would make little sense. Nevertheless, three lessons may be drawn from the Chinese experience. First, China's reform model simply demonstrates that there are different ways of carrying out economic transition but all require sustained political support and sound policy continuity. Second, China's drive to "Reform and Opening Up" originates from a sense of urgency shared by the senior Chinese leadership that their economy was lagging far behind those of its East Asian neighbours because of the inefficiency of command planning and the "closed-door" policy. Third, and related to this, the relative success of China's reform strategy, based on the "open-door" policy and coastal development strategy, can be best understood in connection with economic development and structural change in the Asia-Pacific region since the mid-1980s.

China's Open-Economy Reforms: An Incomplete Process

Despite its large domestic market, the opening up of the Chinese economy has led to a substantial increase in the trade-to-GDP ratio (from less than 5 per cent in 1978 to nearly 20 per cent in 1991). Prior to the 1978 reform, trade was merely a balancing factor to fill gaps in supply and demand under national plans. Once the reform process had begun, and as decentralisation and opening up of the Chinese economy continued, virtually every aspect of China's economic management system had to change as well.

The initial focus of China's economic reform was, however, on *internal* development — the development of import-substituting industries and the agricultural sector. China's foreign-trade and investment regimes were thus strongly inward-looking at the inception of reform. It is since the mid-1980s that China's development strategies have shifted significantly in favour of export production. This corresponds to China's *de facto* adoption of the coastal development strategy, active encouragement of foreign direct investment through various fiscal incentives and the beginning of a large, real devaluation of the Chinese yuan. As a result, China's export structure has increasingly resembled those of Asian NIEs specialising in exports of labour-intensive products.

Over the past years of economic transition, China has established markets for goods and services in which prices are determined by participants in the exchange process. Access to these markets is still limited, however. In addition, the clear rules and regulations needed to prevent the abuse of market power have yet to be established. Thus the markets that exist in China generate rents for those with privileged access to them, and people with good *guanxi* (connections) can ensure that the rents accrue to themselves.

In order to sustain both the reform process and rapid growth in the coming years, it is necessary for China to pursue its open-economy reforms, including:

- the extension of direct trading rights to all enterprises;
- convertibility, if only on the current account;
- continued import liberalisation;
- development of open and competitive markets in intermediate and capital goods and factors of production;
- the establishment of transparent and automatic regulations for foreign direct investment, and
- the removal of discriminatory policies in favour of investment in SEZs and other zones.

Such policies could be expected to remove a good deal of distortion in China's foreign trade, exchange and investment regimes which are a source of monopoly rents and corruption.

China and the OECD Countries

China's entry into the world market is a "positive-sum" game, as it provides new market opportunities for both OECD Member countries and Asian NIEs. Given the strong protectionist sentiment prevailing in part of the OECD area, it is important that OECD Member countries take a balanced view of China's economic transition and growth, taking into account their significance for economic dynamism in the Asia-Pacific region and the world economy as whole. Fear of China's rapid export growth arises from its sheer size, promoting an assumption that "China's exports might soon gobble up the OECD countries' market". However, this supposition tends to overstate the dislocation impact of China's exports on the economies of OECD countries, while understating the positive impact of increased Chinese demand on both regional and world economies. To make China's transition process sustainable, it is crucial for OECD Member countries to keep their markets open. At the same time, the OECD itself could play a more active role in collecting and disseminating up-to-date information among its Member countries regarding the development of China's economic reform.

Chapter 1

Introduction

Since late 1978 China has been introducing reforms that have changed the orientation of its industrialisation drive, usually referred to as China's "opening up" to the outside world. This has allowed China to exploit opportunities provided by access to foreign capital, technology and markets. Macroeconomic figures indicate that China is one of the most dynamic economies in the world; its gross domestic product (GDP) increased by 10 per cent per annum in real terms over the 1981-90 period (Asian Development Bank, 1993). Although its growth rate decelerated sharply in 1989-91 due to anti-inflationary policies, China has resumed double-digit rates of growth since 1992[1].

China's rapid growth in the post-1978 period has been accompanied by even higher growth of merchandise exports. In terms of value, China's merchandise exports quadrupled between 1980 and 1991, surpassing $70 billion and matching the export level of the Republic of Korea (hereafter, Korea). According to the World Bank (1992), China's merchandise exports grew at an annual average rate of 14 per cent in real terms over the same period, exceeding the annual growth rate of Korea's merchandise exports (11 per cent). China is emerging as a leading Pacific economy and entering the ranks of the world's leading traders, together with four Asian NIEs (Newly Industrialising Economies), i.e. Hong Kong, Korea, Singapore and Taiwan[2]. Much of this success is due to the rapid expansion of manufactured exports[3]. Nearly 90 per cent of the increase in total merchandise exports between 1981 and 1991 was accounted for by manufactured goods[4]. For the first two years of the 1990s, the value of China's merchandise exports increased by 17 per cent per annum to reach $85 billion in 1992[5].

Within a relatively short period of 15 years, China has managed to transform itself from an underdeveloped economy into one of the fast-growing NIEs, and its economic management has been gradually shifting from command planning to a market-based economy. Its growth performance and reform experience in the post-1978 period have stirred a debate among policy-makers and economists over what policy advice should be given to the transforming economies in eastern Europe and the former Soviet Union as well as those in Asia and elsewhere. What lessons, if any, can be learned from the Chinese experiment of economic transition to an open economy[6]? At the same time, China's rapid economic growth, led by a strong export performance, has aroused growing concern among established exporters in both developed and developing countries over increased competitive pressures in the world market. What would happen to the "outside world" if China's exports were to continue to grow at their current pace[7]? In some OECD countries, especially in Europe where rising unemployment is an acute political and economic issue, there are serious concerns over competitive pressures from the Asia-Pacific region in general and from China in particular. This situation has given rise to misconceived, protectionist views, which assume that trade with low-wage countries such as China destroys more jobs than it creates[8]. Other developing economies of the Asia-Pacific region have also indicated some concern over China's export competitiveness. This monograph aims to provide a better understanding of China's open-economy reforms since 1978 and the implications of China's entry into the world market for the OECD countries as well as for the developing economies in the Asia-Pacific region.

Scope and Structure of the Study

Over the past decade there have been major changes in China's role in the world economy and in its relationships with economies in the Asia-Pacific region. From a global point of view, China's entry into the world market can be seen as the emergence of a major supplier of labour-intensive products, competing directly with several East and Southeast Asian economies. This development has also added to the pressure for adjustment in the OECD countries. One form of positive adjustment by these established exporters is increased foreign investment in China, directly or via Hong Kong. As will be seen in Chapter III, foreign-funded enterprises have come to play a key role as a vehicle for promoting China's foreign trade; they accounted for a quarter of China's total trade (exports and imports) in 1992[9].

From a regional point of view, China's "coastal development strategy" has brought about the emergence of a "greater Chinese economy" comprising China, Hong Kong and Taiwan[10]. Hong Kong serves as the region's commercial, financial and information centre, through which China's southern provinces have become increasingly integrated with the fast-growing East Asian economies. Taiwan is also emerging as a major source of foreign investment, linking the Chinese mainland to the outside world. The rapid development of coastal provinces such as Guangdong and Fujian has been made possible through the establishment of formal and informal commercial networks with Chinese entrepreneurs located overseas and in Hong Kong, as well as in Taiwan and Southeast Asia[11]. According to recent projections by Armington and Dadush (1993), in purchasing-power parity terms, the "greater Chinese economy" should become the world's largest economic area by the year 2002.

How has China managed to avoid the "supply failure" that other reforming economies, especially those in eastern Europe and the former Soviet Union, have suffered during the process of transition from command planning to a market-based economy? Many economic and political factors seem to have helped bring about a strong "supply response", even at the early stage of reforms. Most observers agree that early success in agrarian reforms based on the introduction of the household responsibility system, together with a relatively stable political structure, set a sound foundation for the overall economic reform in China. However, it is not yet well understood how important "open-economy reforms" have been in enabling China to achieve high economic growth while moving gradually towards an open market economy.

In December 1978, when economic reform was first introduced, China's links with the world economy were subject to highly centralised control. The reform measures introduced at that time concentrated on a liberalisation of these links. The measures, known collectively as the "opening-up" policy, were formulated with respect to (a) the foreign-trade and exchange regimes, (b) the foreign investment regime and (c) the establishment of four Special Economic Zones (SEZs). While all three areas of open-economy reforms have undergone constant change since their inception, some of their characteristics have remained stable throughout. In the area of foreign trade and exchange, these include:

– the removal of controls and devolution of the management of exports, and to a lesser extent imports, away from the centre to provincial and municipal agencies and an increasing number of individual firms, and

– the introduction of a more flexible system for the management of foreign exchange.

In the area of foreign investment, the measures include:

– allowing private investment, including foreign investment, after three decades of prohibition;

– the introduction of rules and regulations to facilitate capitalist management practices, and

– the establishment of a set of fiscal and other incentives to attract foreign investors.

In the third area, the measures involve:

– allowing market-economy practices in China's centrally planned economy, though on a restricted geographical basis, initially on an experimental basis in SEZs established for that purpose[12].

Experience with the measures taken as open-economy reforms has been mixed. In some areas the liberalisation process has continued throughout, while in other areas reaction has led to some backtracking. In addition, the effectiveness of the measures has been varied, with the ostensible liberalisation of some being muted or even neutralised by the fact that they are set in the context of a command economy. In the terminology of one observer, the stance of the reform rhetoric is not the same thing as reform of the system itself: while the rhetoric is quite liberal, in many aspects the actual system is not (Howe, 1990)[13].

One may wonder how China has managed to achieve such rapid growth despite the apparently partial nature of the open-economy reforms implemented so far. What role have these opening-up measures played in the development of the Chinese economy? To answer these questions, it is important to place China's past reforms in a proper perspective. In the following chapter, we examine China's opening-up process since late 1978 from the institutional and administrative points of view. The focus is on changes in the foreign-trade and investment regimes as well as on the development of the Special Economic Zones. Subsequently, we analyse the implications of the emergence of China as a leading Pacific economy from both global and regional points of view. We conclude by discussing the main features of China's open-economy reforms and examining some policy implications of China's entry into the world market for OECD countries and the developing economies in the Asia-Pacific region.

Before getting into the details of China's open-economy reforms, however, it is necessary to touch upon the political aspect of economic reform in China. In this regard, the 14th National Congress of the Chinese Communist Party (CCP), held in October 1992, is considered to be an important milestone. This is not just because it was the first National Congress of the CCP after the Tiananmen Square events on 4 June 1989. It is also because Deng Xiaoping and his reformist followers used this occasion to lay the foundation for consolidating the achievements of 14 years of reform and establishing their legitimacy as a basis for further transition towards an open market economy. A key aspect of the 14th National Congress was that it was successful in putting economic reform before Marxist ideology, dropping two hard-line members (Song Pin and Yao Yilin, both elevated from the State Planning Commission) from the Standing Committee of the Politburo, and appointing three new ones, including Deputy Premier Zhu Rongji, a former mayor of Shanghai and the leading figure of China's economic reform[14].

According to the report delivered by General Secretary Jiang Zemin at the 14th National Congress of the CCP, China will be exploring a new way in which market forces will be given full play. He stated:

> . . . the objective of the reform of the economic structure will be to establish a *socialist market economy* that will further liberate and expand the productive forces. By establishing such an economic structure we mean to let market forces, under the macroeconomic control of the state, serve as the basic means of regulating the allocation of resources, to subject economic activity to the law of value and to make it responsive to the changing relations between supply and demand. We should make use of pricing and competition to distribute resources to those enterprises that yield good economic returns. In this way, we shall provide an incentive for enterprises to improve their performance, so that the efficient ones will prosper and the inefficient ones will be eliminated (*Beijing Review*, Vol. 35, No. 43, 1992, p. 18; emphasis added by the authors).

The concept of socialism was fundamentally modified at the 14th Congress. The new ideology of a "socialist market economy" was first proposed by Deng Xiaoping during his tour to South China in the spring of 1992. He pointed out that:

> . . . a planned economy was not socialism — there was planning under capitalism too. A market economy was not capitalism — there was market regulation under socialism too. Planning and market regulation . . . were both means of controlling economic activity. Whether the emphasis was on planning or on market regulation was not the essential distinction between socialism and capitalism (*Beijing Review*, Vol. 35, No. 43, 1992, p. 17).

Deng Xiaoping's remarks were aimed at legitimising what China had achieved for the last 14 years with the introduction of the "Reforms and Opening Up" policy in late 1978. His remarks also reflect the Chinese authorities' ambitions for the future, that is, China's desire to pursue rapid economic development based on a market economy, while maintaining the political dictatorship of the CCP at the same time. Whether China will be able to manage to "decouple" economic freedom from political freedom remains, of course, an open question.

Nevertheless, one thing that became clear to everyone at the conclusion of the 14th National Congress of the CCP is that no one wants to turn the clock back to the old system of a command economy. The 15 years of reforms have certainly brought visible economic benefits to Chinese people. At the same time, they have learned at a high cost that the management of a market economy is no easy thing on its own. This is particularly true for transitional economies such as China's, in which effective systems of macroeconomic management and resource allocation have yet to be established.

The reform agenda, whose aim is to establish a socialist market economy by the end of this century, was adopted by the Third Plenary Session of the 14th Central Committee of the CCP in November 1993. It is a very ambitious agenda, proposing a wide-ranging reform of China's economic and social structures, covering, amongst others, state-owned enterprises, macroeconomic management, resource allocation, income distribution and social security. It is indeed a formidable challenge for the Chinese leaders to push forward institutional reforms such as the reform of state-owned enterprises without compromising the country's political stability, since these enterprises still remain the main provider of a social safety net in China.

Notes and References

1.   In 1992, the growth rate of China's real GDP was estimated at 12.8 per cent, following 7.7 per cent in 1991. During the first six months of 1993 the economy was growing at an annual rate of close to 14 per cent. Consequently, concern over an overheated economy has recently led the Chinese authorities to cool down the economy by raising interest rates, controlling credit expansion and restricting development zones and property dealings.

2.   In 1992, the value of China's merchandise exports and imports amounted to $85 billion and $80.6 billion, respectively, and ranked 11th and 13th amongst the world's largest exporters and importers. (GATT, *International Trade 92-93: Statistics*, Table I.4., forthcoming).

3.   The relative importance of agriculture as a source of export earnings has declined steadily since the beginning of the 1970s. Agricultural products accounted for more than half of China's export earnings prior to 1970, but by 1987, that share was down to 20 per cent (Anderson, 1990).

4.   Based on the *China Statistical Yearbook*, 1981 and 1992. It should be noted, however, that the *net* contribution of manufactures to the overall growth of China's merchandise exports tends to be overstated, as the value-added component of manufactured exports in China is generally lower than that of primary exports. For a detailed discussion of trade statistics used in this study, see Chapter III.

5.   During the first three quarters of 1993, the growth of China's merchandise exports slowed down to 6.6 per cent over the same period of the previous year (*People's Daily*, overseas edition, 13 October 1993). This may be attributed to the slower growth of China's export markets, combined with the current economic boom at home.

6.   See Gelb, Jefferson and Singh (1993), McMillan and Naughton (1993), Perkins (1992) and Rana and Dowling (1993).

7.   See Hughes (1991, 1992) for a detailed discussion of "export pessimism".

8.   See, for example, the following press articles: "The Sleeping Giant Awakes" (*Financial Times*, 28 June 1993) and "Fortress Mentality" (*Time*, 5 July 1993).

9.   According to the *People's Daily* (overseas edition), 29 September 1993, as of the end of 1992, there were 13 440 foreign-funded enterprises operating in China, which provided 3.4 million jobs, contributed 6 per cent of total industrial output and accounted for investment of $45 billion.

10.   The official announcement of the "coastal development strategy" was made in January 1988 by Zhao Ziyang, former General Secretary of the Chinese Communist Party. In

practice, however, China decided to "open up" 14 cities in the coastal regions in early 1984.

11. See, for example, Vogel (1989).

12. See, for example, Oborne (1986) and Wall (1992a).

13. See also Kleinberg (1990).

14. On 18 October 1992, the CCP's 14th National Congress elected a new Central Committee, consisting of 189 full members and 130 alternates. Nearly half of the elected members were replaced by younger and better educated ones. On the following day, the 14th Central Committee chose a 22-member Politburo at its first Plenary Session as well as seven men for its Standing Committee, the highest decision-making council of the CCP: General Secretary Jiang Zemin, Premier Li Peng, Head of State Security Qiao Shi, former mayor of Tianjin Li Ruihuan, Deputy Premier Zhu Rongji (new), General Liu Huaqing (new) and former Party Secretary of Tibet Hu Jintao (new).

Chapter 2

China's Open-Economy Reforms, 1979-92

Background

The years since 1976 have seen major changes in the political economy of China. The process of establishing a political climate conducive to reform and liberalisation began with the reinstatement of Deng Xiaoping. However it was not until late 1978 that he won the political struggle against Hua Guofeng, who had become new Chairman of the Chinese Communist Party (CCP) following the death of Mao Zedong on 9 September 1976 and the termination of the reign of the "Gang of Four" in October 1976.

During 1978, various speeches by political leaders stressed that the achievement of the Four Modernisations — of agriculture, industry, science and technology and national defense — would require the encouragement of investment by foreigners in the Chinese economy and the importation of foreign technology. Major training programmes for scientists and engineers in China and in the West were announced during the year. The process of liberalisation was consolidated at the landmark Third Plenary Session of the 11th Central Committee of the CCP held in December 1978. At this meeting of the CCP it was announced that:

> Carrying out the Four Modernisations requires great growth in the productive forces, which in turn requires diverse changes in those aspects of the relations of production and superstructure not in harmony with the growth of the productive forces, and requires changes in all methods of management, actions and thinking which stand in the way of such growth. Socialist modernisation is therefore a profound and extensive revolution (*China Quarterly*, 1979, as quoted in Spence, 1990, p. 656).

Although the slogan "the Four Modernisations" was first used by Zhou Enlai in 1964, the policies thought necessary to achieve these objectives, and their political implications, were quite different in 1978. Indeed, this represented a major change in economic-policy thinking in the People's Republic of China (PRC). This shift away from the Maoist economic management system was to have profound implications for all sections of the Chinese people. To make the modernisations possible, the CCP's Central Committee called for the economic control of the Party to be decentralised, greater independence given to local governments, and managerial responsibility turned over to economic units, including factories and farms. It also called for a greater role to be given to prices and for the introduction of free markets ("village fairs") in the rural sector. It also recognised the importance of creating a legal framework and independent judicial institutions to ensure the success of the reforms. The Central Committee believed that it would be possible to achieve the Four Modernisations within the context of the Four Cardinal Principles: socialism, the people's democratic dictatorship, the leadership of the CCP and the guidance of the "universal principles of Marxism-Leninism-Mao-Zedong thought" (*China Quarterly*, 1979, as quoted in Spence, 1990, p. 658). While the Plenary Session was still under way, the significance of the reforms was underscored by the announcement that Coca-Cola had reached an agreement to open a bottling plant in Shanghai and sell its products in China.

The two most important aims of the reforms, in terms of adaptations of the economic management system, were decentralisation of China's centrally planned economy and reversal of the policy of international economic isolation. However, in an economy in the process of transition from a centrally planned economy to one in which market forces are to play an important role, all policy changes are interdependent and mutually reinforcing.

The results of opening up an economy to the outside world are determined by the extent to which decision-makers who relate to that world are affected by domestic policy changes. Their ability to take advantage of international opportunities will be improved by the lifting of constraints on their freedom of action in the domestic economy. Their willingness to do so will be increased if reforms in domestic policies link rewards to action. The 1978 reforms did both. Decentralisation increased the range of individuals and enterprises able to respond to international signals, and liberalisation of domestic factor and goods markets enhanced their ability to do so. Changes to the incentive structure also meant that it was an attractive proposition for individuals and enterprises to engage in international economic activities.

Reforms and Opening Up

The changes in the economic management system set in motion at the Third Plenary Session of the 11th Central Committee of the CCP in December 1978 are known in China as the "Reforms and Opening Up". The "Reforms" are the policy changes which have introduced decentralisation and moves towards more reliance on market forces. "Opening Up" refers to the policy changes aimed at increasing the integration of the Chinese economy into the international economy. This study is concerned with the "Opening Up" process, i.e. the changes in the commercial policy framework that exposes the economy to foreign influences. The impact of those changes, however, cannot be fully understood without some awareness of the "Reforms", which were implemented in the rest of the economy.

The 1978 meeting of the 11th Central Committee can be seen as having passed the political enabling legislation that made it possible to introduce the liberalising economic policy measures. There have been many detailed reforms to economic policy since 1978[1]. They can be grouped into three main categories: those concerned with the ownership of the means of production and the system of economic management; those concerned with the decentralisation of decision-making; and those concerned with price reforms and the establishment of markets.

Ownership and management reforms have involved the establishment of limited tenure rights in agriculture, the establishment of a private sector (Wang, 1991, p. 16), encouragement of the co-operative sector and the merging of some state industries into enterprise groups. Under the contract responsibility system, these enterprises and unreformed state enterprises have been given more discretion over the use of the resources at their disposal, in particular by the replacement of the central collection of all profits with a tax system.

The significance of *decentralisation* is that the productive units owned by provincial and municipal governments, and by central ministries, departments and agencies are no longer rigidly tied to the planning process but have some discretion over what to produce and where to sell.

In the area of *price reforms*, many price controls have been lifted. For many products, however, the decontrol has only been partial: they are subject to dual pricing, with one controlled price, as required under the residual command economy, and one set in the marketplace. The freeing, or partial freeing, of prices combined with decentralisation and economic management reforms has led to the establishment of markets, both retail and wholesale, for consumer and producer goods and factors of production. These markets have partially or completely replaced state distribution systems, or operate in direct competition with them.

The domestic reforms and the easing of political constraints were especially important in determining the consequences of the opening-up process, which the CCP's Central Committee considered necessary to ensure the successful achievement of the Four Modernisations. The willingness and ability of firms in China to trade successfully and efficiently, and of foreigners to invest successfully in China were conditioned as much by reforms in domestic economic policies as by changes in commercial policy, exchange-rate policy and policy towards foreign direct investment.

As noted above, the report of the 1978 Plenary Session did not in itself set out the reforms. It was in essence an "enabling act", giving the green light to the ministries to suggest to the State Council legislation to effect the reforms. The legislative and administrative orders establishing rules and regulations for implementating the reforms came later, though the pace of reform was such that these often followed developments rather than instituted them.

The legislative programme necessary to support the "Reforms" and "Opening Up" process was set out in the Ten Year Development Plan published late in 1978. This Plan set ambitious targets for the growth of trade and for the growth of foreign investment in the Chinese economy. The legislation and administrative orders to ensure the achievement of these targets began to pour out early in 1979. Since then, it has been a continuous process as problems were encountered that needed attention, and as circumstances changed. Keeping track of the constant outflow is difficult. Not all problems have been effectively overcome, however, and the achievement of some targets has been compromised. In what follows, we examine the policy developments in the "Opening Up" process and assess the "quality" of these developments in three main areas: the foreign-trade and exchange regimes, the foreign-investment regime, and the Special Economic Zones.

Foreign-Trade and Exchange Regimes

The Starting Point

China has never had an autarchic economy. Immediately prior to the commencement of economic reforms in 1978, exports accounted for 4.5 per cent of GNP and imports for 4.7 per cent, compared to 6.5 and 8.5 per cent, respectively, for the United States. By 1991, the opening up of the economy had seen China's export-to-GDP ratio rise to 19.6 per cent and its import-to-GDP ratio to 18.6 per cent, far ahead of the United States' 7.4 and 8.9 per cent, respectively[2]. However, while trade has always played an important role in the Chinese economy, this economy cannot be described as an outward-oriented economy, either before the 1978 reforms or right after. The focus of the reforms was on *internal* development, and market forces played a limited role in determining the level and structure of trade.

Prior to the reforms, trade was simply a balancing item in the national plan. The planning process identified shortfalls of essential goods in the domestic economy and determined that the gaps should be filled by imports. More than 90 per cent were producer goods. Exports to generate the foreign exchange to pay for the imports were simply written into the production plans of those sectors whose output was not earmarked in the plan for domestic consumption. More than half of all exports were primary products.

The management of all trade called for in the plans was placed in the hands of foreign trade corporations (FTCs) associated with the producing ministries. The number of FTCs, always small, varied from time to time, but by 1978 there were twelve, controlling all imports into and exports out of China. There were no efficiency tests to ensure that exports were consistent with China's comparative advantage. Production for exports was simply defined as surplus to domestic needs according to the plan and enterprises were required to make available that amount to FTCs. If the producers ran into production difficulties, they were required to give priority to delivering their quotas to FTCs.

Producers sold their supplies to FTCs at domestic prices. FTCs exported at world market prices and were required to sell all the foreign exchange they received to the Bank of China at the official exchange rate. This might or might not amount to the sum that the FTCs had paid to the producers, but as the foreign exchange rate was maintained at an overvalued rate, the FTCs mostly made domestic currency losses on their export activities. Such losses were normally covered by profits on the sales of imports into the domestic market, the overvaluation working in the opposite way in this case. Losses on export trade were either balanced on a cross-subsidy basis within each FTC or by the Ministry of Foreign Trade (later the Ministry of Foreign Economic Relations and Trade, MOFERT, and now the Ministry of Foreign

Trade and Economic Co-operation, MOFTEC) amongst the FTCs and for the system as a whole.

As of 1964 all imports were required to be sold on the domestic market at prices comparable (with quality adjustments) to the prices being charged on the domestic market for similar domestically produced goods. In the 1960s and 1970s this accounted for about 80 per cent of all merchandise imports. The remaining 20 per cent of imports, for which there were no comparable domestic products, were priced on a "cost plus" basis, the "plus" including taxes, tariffs and an exchange-rate premium designed to balance the books of the trading activity by increasing profits from importing sufficiently to cover the losses made on exports. Initially this exchange-rate premium was 103 per cent, staying at this rate from 1964 until 1975. In 1975 it was reduced to 60 per cent, but as this resulted in losses for the FTCs it was increased to 80 per cent in 1977, a rate that was maintained until the system was abolished in 1980 (Lardy, 1992, p. 22). This premium, effectively a limited devaluation of the yuan, offered protection to the development of newly built, import-substituting industries. This system of breaking the links between the domestic and foreign prices of imports and exports, and of insulating exporters and importers from their customers was described by the World Bank (1988, iv) as an "airlock" system.

Decentralising Trade Controls

As with the treatment of foreign investment, to be examined in the next section, the laws and associated regulations governing China's foreign-trade regime have been undergoing more or less constant change since 1978. A main area of China's trade reforms concerns decentralising trade controls. After the 1978 reforms, planning for foreign trade has taken two forms, command planning and guidance planning. The former type is mandatory and set out in physical quantities. On the export side, individual producers are given specific quotas and supplied with the necessary inputs under the materials allocation system for export producers. In 1988, 112 export commodities were covered by the plan, only 21 of which were directly controlled by the State Planning Commission (Lardy, 1992, pp. 40-41). The relative importance of command planning in China's exports was further reduced in subsequent years[3]. As a result, the amount of exports covered by the national plan fell from 100 per cent of total exports in 1978 to 45 per cent in 1988, and down to about 15 per cent in 1992 (Lardy, 1992; World Bank, 1993a, p. 28).

On the import side, a system of "unified management" was introduced in 1984 to control trade in seven key commodities: steel, chemical fertilizers, rubber, timber, tobacco, grain and polyester and other synthetic fibres. Taken together, they accounted for 40 per cent of China's total imports at that time, down from more than 90 per cent at the beginning of the 1980s (Lardy, 1992; World Bank, 1988, p. 22). Further progress was made in scaling down the role of command planning in imports, and in 1992 imports controlled by mandatory plans stood at 18.5 per cent of China's total imports.

The second form of trade planning is "guidance planning". About 20 per cent of exports were subject to guidance planning in 1988. It involved the setting of value targets for decentralised FTCs which were then given a fair degree of flexibility to decide how to meet them. The remaining 35 per cent of exports were managed by independent enterprises, mainly those involving some foreign funding.

Guidance planning on the import side (covering about 30 per cent of all imports) was essentially a foreign-exchange allocation mechanism for imported raw materials, spare parts and capital goods for key investment projects (World Bank, 1988, p. 22, and 1993a, p. 25). The remaining 30 per cent of imports in 1988 were outside the plan and were brought in under license by provincial and municipal governments and by enterprises using foreign exchange they had earned under the retention system, bought on the swap markets, borrowed abroad, or received from abroad as equity finance.

Although the share of trade covered by mandatory trade has been reduced, this does *not* mean that a significant proportion of China's trade is now market-determined. In the first place, the guidance plans can, and often do in effect become mandatory plans when passed on by provincial and municipal governments to their trade corporations. Even the commerce carried out by joint ventures as direct traders is subject to extensive intervention and determined as much by such intervention as by market forces. Possibly, only processing trade based on international subcontracting and border trade in existing stocks of products can be regarded as being determined predominantly by market forces. Most trade, even if organised on a decentralised basis, remains subject in one way or another to a planning process[4]. Only when the profits and losses of individual trade flows accrue to, or are borne by, the agents directly involved in that trade and when price reforms result in input prices reflecting market values, will China's international trade flows be fully determined by market forces.

China's highly centralised control over foreign trade began to give way to a more diffused regime early in 1978, with foreign trade corporations (FTCs) in Guangdong province beginning to act independently of the centre (Vogel, 1989, pp. 348ff). During 1979 many local FTCs began to engage in trade in their own right. The practice was officially sanctioned and legislation soon followed to authorise entities other than the twelve national FTCs to engage in trade. Central ministries and departments and provincial and municipal governments established their own FTCs, some being domestic joint ventures involving production units and trading corporations: by the mid-1980s over 800 FTCs had been authorised and by the end of the 1980s more than 5 000 were in operation. In addition to the FTCs owned by the governments, large state-owned enterprises, initially those with exports in excess of $750 000, were given the right to export on their own account, as in the case of foreign-funded enterprises[5].

However, the decentralisation of the *process* of trading does not mean that trade was becoming market-determined in the same proportion. Trade in products covered by mandatory plans was still highly centralised and that covered by guidance plans still subject to tight controls. Trade above plan targets for products covered by the guidance plan and in "third category" products outside the plan was more open to determination by incentives, but such trade was still not conducted in a free market environment. Permission to import was still rigidly controlled by licensing, and export procurement was still carried out in the price "airlock" and still subject to government control of resource allocation in factor and intermediate goods markets.

Thus, even a decade after the reforms began, the principle of independent accounting and responsibility for FTCs to assume any profits and losses from foreign-trade activities was not fully realised. The main incentive for the decentralised trade corporations and enterprises to engage in exporting was not profit but access to foreign exchange. Under the system of foreign-exchange retention in operation in China (see below), exporters have the right to retain access to some of the proceeds of their export activities. This was in addition to any allocations received under the plan. Involvement in exporting also allowed trade corporations and enterprises to build up illegal holdings of foreign exchange abroad through such arrangements as distorted transfer pricing and inflated commissions. As losses that were not covered by profits from imports were covered by local, provincial or central governments (sometimes indirectly by the banking sector), trade corporations and enterprises would export whatever products over which they could gain control. They would then seek whatever prices they could obtain without considering whether or not the exporting made economic sense in itself. The objective was to gain access to foreign exchange at any price.

Contract Responsibility System

In an attempt to prevent exports from being dumped abroad at a loss and to limit government fiscal commitments, the government applied the *contract responsibility system* to foreign trade in 1988 for national FTCs. It was extended to provincial governments in 1991. The intentions were to remove the open-ended commitment of the central government to subsidise exports on the one hand, and to relate domestic prices of exports increasingly to those being obtained on world markets on the other. The contracts specified targets for foreign-exchange earnings, remittances of foreign exchange from the FTCs — both provincial and national — to the centre, and the balance of profits and losses from trade activities. The last target implied that the central government was prepared to accept the responsibility of subsidising some exports; any losses above these were to be covered by FTCs or provincial governments themselves. Then, as the national and provincial FTCs in turn signed contracts with subsidiary bodies, this commitment to cover losses on trade was partly taken on by them and partly passed on to the lower-level entities.

As exchange rates continued to be overvalued (despite reforms in the foreign-exchange market) the incentive to export at a loss continued. However, instead of all of the cost being passed on to the central government, some was now covered by "cross subsidy" by the local governments, FTCs, and export enterprises themselves. These cross subsidies came, for example, from the profits from imports imported at overvalued exchange rates and sold into the highly protected domestic market. Bank finance to cover the losses was also increasingly resorted to. Thus, while the burden of financing export subsidies was redistributed, the practice itself continued. Similarly, the wedge driven between international and domestic prices by the distorted exchange rates, trade protection and the unreformed price system remained in place.

In December 1990 the State Council announced that as of 1 January 1991, trade contracts would not be allowed to contain provisions for direct subsidies on exports. However, as the only other relevant reform enacted was one that reduced the benefits of the foreign exchange retention system, many exporters have continued to take and accept losses. The losses now have to be covered, as indicated above, by cross subsidies from import trade within the enterprise or by increased bank "borrowing".

Agency System

The decentralised contract-responsibility system for exporters, complete with its continued flow of losses on much export trade and protection-engendered profits on import trade, did nothing on its own to remove the "airlock" between domestic and world market prices. The traditional method involved the FTCs buying from domestic producers at domestic prices and selling at world market prices for exports, vice versa for imports, with the FTCs keeping the profits or absorbing the losses. One reform was designed to overcome this and bring the two sets of prices more closely into line. This was the introduction of the *agency system*, which was approved by the State Council in 1984. Under this system, the wedge, or "airlock", between domestic prices and international prices was to be removed. FTCs would simply act as agents for producers of export goods or consumers of imports. They would pass on the international price, in both cases converted via the exchange rate, and add on a service charge and any taxes payable. Thus, domestic producers and consumers were to be directly linked to the prices on the international market. The agency fee was set at cost for Chinese clients, but closer to what the market would bear for foreign-funded enterprises.

The use of the agency system was adopted quickly for imports, covering almost all capital goods and about three-quarters of total imports by 1992. For exporters, however, the agency system only makes sense for exports that are profitable in themselves and more so than selling on the domestic market, and whose producers do not have the option of exporting directly. The continued combination of overvalued exchange rates, other cost-raising distortions in the domestic price system and the existence of a profitable protected domestic market means that less use has been made of the agency system for exports — roughly 10 per cent by 1990.

Commercial Policy

As noted earlier, prior to the 1978 reforms, China's foreign trade was conducted by the twelve national foreign-trade corporations (FTCs) in accordance with the national plan. In that context there was no need for commercial policy. Such tariffs as did exist were purely for revenue-raising purposes. As commercial policy instruments they were redundant. Decisions to import or export were taken in accordance with the plan, and prices or quantities were set at domestic levels, as discussed above. As decentralisation of trade took place and as imports were recategorised into those subject to mandatory planning, those subject to a guidance plan and those outside of the plan, it was necessary to develop a commercial policy to provide a policy framework for international trade.

As the scope of planning declined, control over trade was increasingly effected by the use of licenses, for both imports and exports. At the peak, imports of

53 product groups (in 1989) and exports of 235 product groups (in 1986) were covered by licenses. This licensed trade accounted for two-thirds of all exports and 46 per cent of imports (Lardy, 1992, p. 44)[6]. Trade not covered by the planning process or licenses is not, however, "free" trade. Enterprises have to submit regular import plans for approval by the authorities and demonstrate in advance that specific import intentions are included in those plans. Without that approval they cannot use their foreign-exchange entitlements or buy such entitlements (or foreign exchange) on the swap markets. In Shenzhen, regulations were introduced in 1992 that allowed foreign-funded enterprises simply to report imports as they were brought in — as long as they were specified in their production plans.

In the absence of a free market in foreign exchange, import licensing has been used, in conjunction with macroeconomic policy instruments, as a balance-of-payments policy instrument. Import licenses have also been applied to provide protection for approved import-substituting industries, particularly those producing consumer durables, especially during the period of the Seventh National Plan (1986-90). On the other hand, export licensing is used to keep prices high in cases where China is a dominant supplier, for example in the fresh-food markets in Hong Kong and Macao and in the world markets for tin, tungsten and antimony. In addition, export licenses have been applied in order to ensure that China keeps its obligations under international agreements such as the Multifibre Arrangement (MFA) and voluntary export restraint agreements.

Quotas under the import and export licenses, and for the Generalized System of Preferences (GSP) are allocated centrally. The quotas are much sought after as they generate substantial rents. The existence of such rents allows the government directly to protect enterprises engaged in import substitution. Other enterprises which are making losses on some activities can be protected indirectly by using them for cross-subsidy purposes.

China is currently seeking to rejoin GATT. As part of the preparations for rejoining, the government has begun the process of reducing the amount of trade covered by mandatory planning and by licenses. By early 1992, 53 broad product groups were covered by import licenses, covering an estimated quarter of all imports. At the same time, tariffs began to be used for trade-policy purposes early in the 1980s. Where domestic production from import-substituting industries was high cost but insufficient to satisfy the home market, tariffs were used to raise the price of imports to domestic levels for protective purposes. Such tariffs were as high as 140 per cent or more in the case of least essential items such as tobacco products. The unweighted average nominal protection rate for the whole economy in 1992 was 42.8 per cent, with the higher rates concentrated on finished consumer goods where the average rate was 65 per cent. China has maintained a "tariff escalation" structure according to the stage of processing. Though it is similar to tariff structures in other developing countries (World Bank, 1993a, p. 57), China's actual tariff revenue collected, relative to total imports, gives a much lower rate of 5.6 per cent in 1992, compared with other developing countries such as India (51.2 per cent in 1986) and Pakistan (30.8 per cent in 1990)[7]. This is because the range of tariff exemptions has become quite extensive (see below).

Tariff exemptions are granted for imports used to produce exports, for import requirements of capital goods by enterprises considered to be raising the level of technology in China, for raw materials and intermediate and capital goods imported into the Special Economic Zones, Economic and Technological Development Zones and for those imported by Sino-foreign joint ventures and co-operative enterprises. Tariffs are also reduced by 50 per cent for consumers in the Special Economic Zones. In addition to these tariff rebates, the government also follows international practice and rebates indirect taxes for exports (except, as already noted, for exports where China considers itself to have a dominant market position, in which case extra taxes and export duties are imposed)[8].

Tariff exemptions and rebates have been an important trade instrument for China's "export push" of manufactured goods in the recent years. Its exports associated with import duty concessions amounted to more than 60 per cent of total manufactured exports in 1991 (World Bank, 1993a, p. 60). However, the combination of access to import duty concessions and a relatively high-cost production of domestic intermediate inputs, which is partly attributable to the existing tariff structure, has resulted in a very low domestic content of China's manufactured exports. Although reliable cost data are scarce and fragmented, there appear to be a number of manufacturing sectors that have negative value added *at world prices* (World Bank, 1993a, pp. 73-75).

In sum, China's commercial policy has been moving away from the prereform "airlock" system in which, as far as prices were concerned, the domestic economy was isolated from the international economy. On a formal level, mandatory planning controls have been reduced and the amount of trade subject to licensing lowered. Tariffication has commenced and a start has been made on reducing the policy bias against exports with a wide-ranging package of tariff exemptions and tax rebates. It is, however, still far from a neutral incentive structure — most enterprises involved in foreign trade are state-owned or collective enterprises, where decisions reflect other things than simply prices.

Foreign-Exchange Policy

Before the 1978 reforms the exchange rate played no role in the determination of China's international trade flows. It simply defined the size of the profits or losses realised by the FTCs from their trading activities. Even after the reforms commenced, this continued to be the case for those products covered by the mandatory plans and also, to some extent, for those covered by guidance planning. However, successive reforms in the exchange-rate mechanism have led to more and more of China's trade being conducted at increasingly market-determined exchange rates.

One early reform, a *de facto* devaluation of the yuan for trade purposes, had little economic impact for most traders. The yuan had traditionally been valued on a purchasing power parity (PPP) basis, which meant that for many years the Chinese currency was overvalued because of distortions in the Chinese price system. In the 1970s the relative price stability of China led to a continuous revaluation of the yuan, from 2.46 to the dollar in 1970 to 1.50 at the end of 1979. In 1981 the government introduced an "internal settlement rate" (ISR) of 2.8 to the dollar for all trade transactions. This represented a shift in the basis of valuing the yuan, at least for trade purposes, from a PPP basis to one based on the cost of earning foreign exchange. The introduction of a devalued rate in a dual exchange-rate system temporarily reversed the situation in which most exports by the FTCs were loss-making, whereas importing was profitable. After the introduction of the ISR, more exports became profitable, or less loss-making, and imports became less profitable. This *de facto* devaluation had a real impact only on importers and exporters using the agency system, or where they were responsible for their own profits and losses. As the share of trade covered by the agency system and own account increased, so, too, did the share of trade for which the new foreign exchange system mattered.

The ISR system proved unsuccessful in reducing the budgetary deficit needed to support the FTCs, nor did it have a significant impact on the development of profitable exports. It was also considered illegal by the IMF and opposed by China's trade partners who considered it a form of export subsidy. In 1984 the official exchange rate was brought into line with the ISR of 2.8 to the dollar. The ISR system itself was abolished in 1985.

A more important reform, the *foreign-exchange retention system*, was put into practice in 1979, two years' earlier than the introduction of the ISR system. Previously all foreign exchange earnings had to be handed over to the Bank of China at the official exchange rate. Allocations of foreign exchange to finance imports were determined by the national plan. The introduction of the retention system meant that exports, and some non-trade activities such as tourism, would generate an entitlement to purchase back, for approved purposes, some proportion of the foreign exchange that had been handed over to the Bank of China. The official exchange rate was used for these transactions. The proportion of earnings subject to retention varied according to the type of activity and the location of the exporter, initially ranging from 5 per cent to 50 per cent. In 1988, the level and range were increased from a minimum of 25 per cent, through 30 per cent for Guangdong and Fujian provinces, to 100 per cent for foreign-funded enterprises in the Special Economic Zones (SEZs), enterprises in Tibet and for the People's Liberation Army (PLA). The entitlement was split between the provincial and local governments, the foreign-trade corporations (FTCs) and the exporter, the share being decided by negotiation.

The range of special retention rates proliferated through the 1980s, producing distortions in resource allocation as enterprises sought to maximise their entitlements to foreign exchange. In January 1991 the State Council announced a major revision to the scheme, reducing the number of basic rates to two: 70 per cent for electrical and capital goods and 50 per cent for everything else (*Far Eastern Economic Review*, 24 January 1991)[9]. Of the 50 per cent submitted to the government, two-fifths was bought in at the official rate and the rest at the more market-determined swap rate (see below). Only foreign-funded enterprises in SEZs, enterprises in Tibet and the PLA are now allowed a 100 per cent retention rate.

The economic value of foreign-exchange entitlements has varied over time. They are valueless if the government does not authorise them to be exchanged for foreign currency. In the early years this permission was often withheld to conserve reserves. In some cases enterprises could not use their entitlements because of a lack of local currency during credit squeezes. In other cases they were requisitioned by the provincial government that owned the enterprise (Sung, 1991, p. 51). By 1985, the value of outstanding entitlements reached $16 billion, that is 1.3 times the value of China's foreign exchange reserves of $11.9 billion (Jiang, 1992). After 1986, when balance-of-payments conditions improved, enterprises could be more confident that they would be able to exchange their entitlements for foreign currency and the incentive effect of the scheme was thus enhanced.

Another determinant of the value of the retention entitlements has been the development of markets in which they can be traded. Such markets were needed to help enterprises with surplus entitlements to sell them to enterprises with deficits — for example, those selling their products only in the domestic market but with requirements for imported capital goods or raw materials for which they were not allocated foreign exchange under the national plan. Initially this trading was carried out by authorised brokers (Oborne, 1986, p. 43). With the rapid growth in the volume of entitlements, especially in the southern provinces, the need for a more institutionalised market developed. In 1981 a foreign exchange trading room was opened in the Bank of China's Guangzhou branch (Vogel, 1989, p. 353) and similar arrangements were set up in Shanghai (Lardy, 1992, p. 58). At first, only Chinese enterprises were allowed access to the markets, but in 1985 a "swap centre" (or foreign-exchange transaction centre) was formally opened in Shenzhen to carry out deals in foreign-exchange entitlements for joint-venture enterprises. Later, such centres were opened in all major commercial centres in China and the right of access to them, though indirect, was continually extended to virtually any entity or individual who had a valid import license or authority for other approved use, for example, student fees or repatriation of profits by import-substituting, foreign-funded enterprises.

Initially the entitlement was to purchase foreign exchange at the internal settlement rate (ISR), but when that was abolished (1985) the rate used was the official rate. As both rates have always been overvalued, the entitlements have almost always carried a premium in the swap centres. For importers this moves the price of imports closer to world market levels, and for exporters it either reduces losses or adds to profits from exporting.

The swap markets are *not* free markets, however. In the first place, access to them is controlled; as already noted, their use requires specific authorisation. The ease with which such authorisation is obtained varies. Second, the foreign exchange covered by the approval has to be spent within six months on the items specified. In addition, various authorities have intervened in the markets at different moments to limit price changes. Despite these constraining factors, the foreign-exchange market in China is freer than at any time since 1949. The reduction in the number of retention rates for Chinese enterprises to two in 1991 and their uniform application across China have also reduced the distortions due to the foreign-exchange retention system. In addition, with the official rate's more or less tracking the swap rate with a narrowing differential — at least until early 1992 — the exchange-rate system was moving towards a unified one. With the freer flow of foreign exchange into the swap market and easier access to it, the gap was also narrowing between the two legal rates and the black-market rate used by those without approval to use the swap market.

While the continued restrictions on access to the markets imply that the yuan remains overvalued, the degree of overvaluation was substantially lessened and consequently, distortions in resource allocation were reduced until early 1992, when the gap once again widened to approximately 40 per cent, reflecting the overheating of the economy. The swap rate reached 8.2 yuan to the dollar in several swap centres in December 1992, while the official rate stood at 5.8 (see Figure II-1).

There have been major developments in China's foreign-exchange market since mid-1993, when the swap rate reached almost 10 yuan to the dollar. The authorities introduced macroeconomic adjustment measures to cool off overheating by raising interest rates, controlling bank loans and restricting business investment in the real-estate sector. As a result of these macroeconomic measures and intervention in the swap-market transactions, the swap rate swung back to a level of around 8.5 yuan. Furthermore, effective on 1 January 1994, the authorities replaced a dual system of exchange rates by a unified exchange-rate system with a managed float against a basket of foreign currencies. This move allowed the official rate to be devalued effectively by 50 per cent to 8.7 yuan to the dollar, in line with the average rate prevailing at foreign-exchange swap markets around the country.

In short, the moves towards convertibility for a growing number of economic entities and the moves towards an equilibrium exchange rate imply that the distortionary impact of the controlled foreign-exchange mechanism has been gradually eliminated and market signals have been coming closer to a reflection of comparative advantage — closer, but not yet there. Many other distortions under the foreign-trade regime continue to exist, maintaining the "airlock" between domestic and world prices.

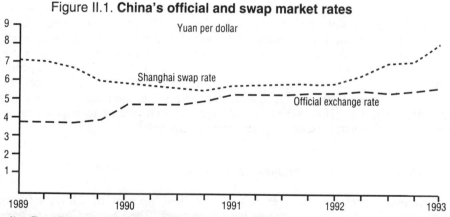

Figure II.1. **China's official and swap market rates**

Note: These figures are quarterly averages of weekly exchange rates.
Source: The Shanghai Swap Center.

Foreign-Investment Regime

Perhaps the most dramatic turnaround brought about by the process of "Reforms and Opening Up" was the shift away from prohibition on foreign direct investment (FDI) in China towards its active encouragement. The primary purpose of this "regime change" was to gain access to modern technology, both embodied and disembodied, packaged with capital, management skills and international networking. Along with this went the hope that the change would generate foreign-exchange earnings from resulting exports, though in practice this has always been a secondary objective. Encouragement of these factors of production in a non-packaged form came much later; portfolio investment in China, for example, was not allowed until 1991, and then only on a very restricted basis.

With respect to FDI, the Chinese authorities often use the term *sanzi qiye* or "foreign-funded (-invested) enterprises", which are of three types: equity joint ventures (JVs), contractual (or co-operative) ventures (CVs) and wholly foreign-owned ventures (FVs)[10]. JVs are limited-liability companies set up jointly by Chinese and foreign parties in accordance with the 1979 Law on Chinese-Foreign Joint Ventures (see below), and profits are distributed according to each party's equity contribution[11].

CV refers to a wide range of contractual arrangements between Chinese and foreign partners involving long-term investment co-operation. At one extreme, CVs may be simply Chinese enterprises that have long-term technical and production co-operation arrangements with foreign firms providing production equipment, technical know-how and marketing expertise in return for profits specified by contract. In these cases, CVs would be almost indistinguishable from non-equity, subcontracting arrangements, and very similar to arrangements such as "processing and assembly operations" or "compensation trade". In the official Chinese statistics, these latter items are recorded under "Other Foreign Investment", as opposed to "Direct Foreign Investment"[12]. At the other extreme, when the financial contribution by the Chinese partners is minimal, CVs would become quite similar to wholly foreign-owned ventures (FVs), except that foreign partners prefer to have "a prior claim to repayment of the initial investment rather than a share in long-term profits" (Pomfret, 1991, p. 36). In the terminology of the official Chinese statistics, FDI includes the three types of foreign-funded enterprises and the so-called joint exploration ventures (JEs), which are the type of FDI related to exploration and development of mineral resources, particularly petroleum[13].

Setting the Legislative Framework

Annex 1 presents an overview of the development of China's foreign investment policy and its concomitant legal framework. The Law on Chinese-Foreign Joint Ventures enacted in July 1979 was the landmark legislation on inward foreign direct investment. This law codified the right of foreign firms to invest in China and to co-operate with Chinese counterparts in various ways; it defined the nature of joint ventures that would be allowed to invest in China. It also began the process of establishing an institutional and administrative framework covering FDI in China.

36

The 1979 Law did *not* prohibit wholly foreign-owned ventures (FVs). There was, however, a residual antipathy amongst conservatives towards foreigners so that relatively few FVs were actually established in the first years of reforms. The permission to foreign investors to establish, which was introduced by the 1979 Law, was later "enshrined" in the 1982 Constitution as Article 18, which offered protection to their "lawful rights and interests" and required them to abide by Chinese laws.

Between 1979 and 1986 several laws aimed at specific issues relating to foreign investment were introduced. With respect to income tax, the Income Tax Law on Joint Ventures was introduced in September 1980, followed by the Income Tax Law on Wholly Foreign-Owned Enterprises in December 1981. In addition to extending the application of standard taxation rules to foreign-funded enterprises, these laws also introduced various tax incentives in the form of tax holidays and concessions. Special incentives to encourage the import of "advanced technology" on preferential terms were also introduced. Moreover, a Civil Procedure Law was enacted in 1986, which established processes for resolving disputes between foreign investors and Chinese counterparts or agencies. The legal framework was further strengthened in April 1985 with the introduction of the Foreign Economic Contract Law, setting out rules for contracts between foreign enterprises and Chinese partners and other entities. In April 1991, tax laws relating to foreign investors were harmonised, establishing uniform income tax rates and preferential terms for foreign-funded enterprises.

Starting from a complete vacuum, it was inevitable that as foreign investment grew, problems would emerge from time to time. As they did, or as patterns of foreign investment emerged that the government wished to discourage, the State Council proposed new legislation to the National Peoples' Congress. For example, in October 1986 major general legislation on foreign direct investment was introduced in response to concern that much investment was using "low technology", concentrated in the service sector (e.g. hotels, restaurants and tourism) and aimed at the domestic market. The "Provisions for Encouragement of Foreign Investment" contain 22 articles, giving it the common name of the "22 Articles law". This represented a turning point in China's policy towards foreign direct investment in that the Chinese authorities differentiated amongst types of FDI and singled out "export enterprises" and "technologically advanced enterprises" for specific encouragement.

The encouragement was provided partly through the removal of obstacles about which existing investors had complained — such as their inability to hire and fire workers in line with the company's needs — and through the introduction of extra tax incentives and privileged access to input materials. Detailed rules to facilitate the implementation of the "22 Articles" were introduced in 1987, as were rules establishing which import-substituting activities could benefit from incentives. In response to the fact that foreign partners in joint ventures (JVs) and contractual ventures (CVs) were not always making an adequate contribution to capital, regulations on Chinese-Foreign Co-operative Enterprises were introduced in 1988. These regulations were designed to prevent the overvaluation of assets provided as the foreign partners' equity, the failure to provide agreed finance or the delivery of machinery different from that agreed upon.

Until 1986, most legislative and political attention had been focused on JVs. However, many CVs involving agreements between Chinese and foreign enterprises had been formed and the number of CVs had increased to more than 5 000 by 1988. The provision of a legal framework for these CVs was finally established when the National People's Congress passed the Law on Co-operative Ventures in April 1988. Earlier, in April 1986, the Congress had also passed the Law on Enterprises Operated Exclusively with Foreign Capital, following political acceptance of the fact that antipathy towards wholly foreign-owned ventures (FVs) was losing China some desirable investment.

Further laws governing foreign investment have continued to be introduced. In April 1988, the Chinese Constitution was revised to ensure the right to lease land to foreign firms. In May 1990, laws liberalising controls on the use of land by foreign investors were also introduced, as were laws allowing the Chairperson of foreign-funded enterprises to be a foreigner. The period over which joint-venture agreements could operate was extended — up to 70 years for some projects. In other cases they are now permitted on an open-ended basis. Moreover, to attract foreign investment from Taiwan, Hong Kong and Macao under the "coastal development strategy", which was already in practice since 1984, specially favourable laws were passed in 1988 and 1990. The year 1992 also saw the introduction of a law to improve protection of intellectual property rights.

In addition to the domestic legislation discussed above, the Chinese authorities have also negotiated bilateral investment agreements with major home countries. The first of bilateral investment treaties was signed up with Sweden in March 1982. As of end 1992 the number of such investment agreements reached 41 countries. Bilateral treaties on the avoidance of double taxation for foreign investors had been signed with 34 countries by mid-1993. These bilateral agreements grant foreign investors in China the right of repatriation and compensation against nationalisation and provide them with protection against double taxation.

Provincial governments and municipalities have also made their own contribution to the legislative environment for foreign-funded enterprises. Incentives relating to land use, preferential local taxes and special institutional arrangements have been added to the national laws. Competition amongst different sites has led to the proliferation of such special concessions[14].

In sum, starting with a blank page, the Government of China has promulgated a wide range of laws and their associated rules and regulations, providing an increasingly comprehensive legal framework for foreign-funded enterprises operating in China. On paper, the laws, rules and regulations — national and local — provide an attractive incentive framework. In the words of one commentator:

> By 1988, the legislated investment incentives compared favourably to those offered by other Asian countries, although there is considerable evidence of non-legislative disincentives to investing in China (Pomfret, 1991, p. 24).

The further changes in foreign investment laws introduced since 1988 have certainly enhanced those incentives.

Incentives and Regulations

The main attractions for foreigners to invest in China are China's absolute and comparative advantages and the existence of a large domestic market. The removal of prohibitions on such investment would probably have been sufficient on its own to stimulate many foreign investors, particularly those seeking to exploit minerals such as oil and coal, and land, both for real estate development and for commercial farming development close to Hong Kong and Macao. Some would have been attracted by China's comparative advantage in cheap labour, others would have been seduced by the dream of exploiting the country's vast domestic market of 1.2 billion people. Whether or not additional incentives were necessary to attract foreign investors is a moot point. After examining the practices and experiences of other Asian countries, however, the Government of China decided to introduce a wide range of incentives, because it *believed* that it needed at least to match those offered by its neighbours, especially Hong Kong and Taiwan.

Incentives for foreign investors fall into two categories. The first are genuine and aim to raise returns from investment above those of other activities. The second are government interventions that simply seek to remove cost-raising obstacles to investment. In a Communist country the latter are probably the more significant, at least in the early stages of reform.

Tax Incentives

The most obvious incentives for foreign investors are tax concessions. These take the form of reduced tax rates, tax holidays, and preferential deductions. China has a very full and very complex set of such concessions. Tax laws introduced in April 1991 removed a discrimination against wholly foreign-owned enterprises and established a common standard corporation tax rate of 33 per cent for all foreign-funded enterprises operating in China, except for those in the 14 Open Coastal Cities[15] and other open areas, where the rate is 24 per cent, and for those in SEZs, ETDZs and the Pudong New Area, where the rate is 15 per cent. These rates contrast with the national 55 per cent imposed on domestic firms, although actual rates of tax *plus* profits remitted to the government by domestic firms are largely negotiable, averaging 58 per cent in 1988, according to the World Bank (1990, Table 3.2, p. 41).

In addition to these tax-rate reductions, there is a plethora of tax holidays and exemptions for foreign-funded enterprises. There is a general tax holiday clause for all such productive (i.e. non-service sector) enterprises engaged in industry, agriculture and animal husbandry with expected operational lives of more than ten years. Such firms have a tax holiday for the first two years in which they make profits net of carried forward losses. They are then allowed a 50 per cent reduction in taxes for the following three years.

There is a threshold criterion for service industries. In these industries the foreign investment component has to be in excess of $5 million. If this additional qualification is met, then such firms are allowed one net profit-making year free of taxes, plus a 50 per cent tax reduction for a further two years. Firms involved in the construction of wharfs and harbours with expected lives greater than 15 are allowed five tax-free years followed by five years at a 50 per cent discount rate. Firms that employ advanced technology have a further three years in which they pay tax at a reduced rate of 10 per cent. Moreover, any firm which, after the expiration of the tax holiday and discount period, exports at least 70 per cent of its production by value will have its tax rate maintained at 10 per cent. Losses can be carried forward for five years.

For foreign firms attracted by China's domestic market, commercial sales (i.e. exports) into that market are subject to normal import duties. For 104 designated product groups a consolidated sales tax is also payable at rates varying between 1.5 per cent and 66 per cent. However, import-substituting firms that can convince the authorities that the technology they use is of an advanced standard are given a two-year holiday from payment of consolidated tax — five years in the case of banks. All firms, domestic and foreign, pay a property tax of 1.2 per cent of the depreciated value of their buildings (including housing), or 18 per cent of the rental value.

How significant these tax concessions are to foreign investors is not clear, however. Some commentators think that they are more or less irrelevant in determining the overall size of foreign investment flows. For example, Pomfret (1991, p. 133) argues that:

> . . . tax holidays and complex incentive packages do not seem to affect the investment decision crucially, although foreign investors will, of course, accept any such benefits if they are offered.

Firms from countries which have signed double taxation agreements with China may in fact prefer to pay Chinese taxes, rather than have to raise the foreign exchange to pay taxes in their home countries. In 1990, tax revenue (exclusive of customs duty) from foreign firms alone — mostly foreign-funded enterprises — amounted to 4.35 billion yuan, less than 2 per cent of national tax revenue. Smaller companies can, and do, adjust their accounts by transfer pricing and payment of "commissions" to reduce tax liabilities, often reporting continuous losses for this reason. The possibility of converting taxes that would otherwise be payable by Chinese enterprises may be the strongest incentive effect, sufficient to stimulate such enterprises into seeking foreign partners for joint ventures.

Foreign-Exchange Retention

As we have seen, a major part of the opening-up process has been the continual easing of access to foreign exchange. Initially this was done through the foreign-exchange retention system. The rates of retention were largely determined by factors such as the nature of the foreign-exchange earning activity, its location and its growth pattern. The scheme did *not* in itself discriminate in favour of foreign-funded enterprises, though the way in which it was operated in the early years did[16]. On the other hand, foreign-funded enterprises could maintain bank accounts in foreign currency. In itself this was only the removal of an impediment and not an "incentive" to invest. However, this concession became an "incentive" when it was combined with the right to sell such holdings for a premium on a swap market less restricted than the official market. This raised the rate of return on foreign-exchange-generating activities for foreign-funded enterprises above that which could be achieved by domestic firms. This incentive was gradually reduced as access to the swap market was widened after 1988. The gap between the official exchange rate and the swap rate diminished and almost disappeared in 1991. However, the premium, and therefore the incentive, reappeared during 1992 when the gap between the two rates widened again by as much as 50 per cent.

One further incentive for joint ventures, which was introduced in 1986, was the right to buy foreign exchange on the swap market out of the *renminbi* proceeds of import-substituting activities, although for some time this right was of limited value as the authorities effectively prevented enterprises from taking advantage of it (Lardy, 1992, p. 62).

Obstacle-Removing Interventions

In addition to the perceived political risks of investing in a Communist-controlled country, early foreign investors complained of many operational problems. Some were related to the underdeveloped infrastructure, in particular communications, transportation and power, while others were related to policy-induced factors inherent in a command economy, such as restricted access to, and restrictions on, the use of land and labour, intermediate goods and raw materials. There have been consistent complaints that to deal with these problems and even to establish joint ventures at all requires considerable effort involving multifarious levels of bureaucracy and political actors. Companies need to join the *guanxi* system to facilitate their successful operations[17]. The Government of China also recognises that enterprises are subject to "random taxation" in the form of *ad hoc* calls for funds from various local government entities and agents of the central government. In the absence of a well-functioning and independent legal system incorporating enforceable commercial law, fear of arbitrary administrative intervention has also acted as a constraint on the growth of at least some forms of foreign investment, such as joint ventures in technologically advanced industries, which are much sought after by the Chinese authorities. This is one reason why Hong Kong and Taiwan, which are familiar with the *guanxi* system, have dominated FDI in China[18].

Branches of the government from the State Council down to municipal government offices have recognised these obstacles to the free development of foreign investment and have made various efforts to overcome them. Investment in infrastructure has been encouraged and priority access to it for foreign investors has been called for. Offices have been established to facilitate the access of foreign-funded enterprises to raw materials and intermediate goods, in some cases to take advantage of the secondary free markets that have developed in these items.

Central legislation and administrative orders have been introduced along with provincial and municipal actions to enable foreign-funded enterprises to cope with the vagaries of dealing with the government mechanisms of a command economy. Such interventions cover, for example, labour mobility, the leasing of land, arbitrary financial impositions[19], "one stop" shops and dispute procedures. It must be acknowledged, however, that as in other formerly command-economy countries

41

undergoing economic liberalisation, the "soft will" of such well-meaning, government-inspired interventions has run up against the "hard will" of the bureaucrats and cadres who operate the government machinery in their own interest. They seek to maintain their rent-generating activities, even if these activities are made illegal. To the extent that the interventions successfully support the liberalisation of the economy, they can and do facilitate the process of foreign investment. Sometimes it is a matter of forming the correct alliances, for example, in the choice of a local joint-venture partner whose *guanxi* is strong enough to make the system work in favour of the enterprise, or of the choice of a location where the political leaders have sufficient standing effectively to support the foreign investors who establish there.

Special Economic Zones

Introduction

The pressures for reform in economic policy that arose after the Cultural Revolution did not go unchallenged. Many leaders of the Communist Party of China were not convinced of the need for the radical shifts being proposed by Deng Xiaoping and his supporters. Apprehension was strongest with respect to the role to be played by foreigners in the economic development of the new China. While the controversy over the reform proposals raged in Beijing in 1978, a Hong Kong-based multinational corporation owned by the Chinese government, China Merchants Steam Navigation Company, proposed that it should be allowed to extend its activities into the mainland. One of its proposals was that it should be authorised to develop a small area of China's border with Hong Kong, collaborating with foreign companies by setting up joint ventures there.

The China Merchants proposal seemed to offer a compromise solution to the problem of how to introduce foreign investors and their capitalist practices into China while limiting the political repercussions of doing so. The idea of allowing such activity in a remote and tightly restricted area proved an acceptable compromise and the establishment of the Shekou Industrial Park took place late in January 1979[20]. In February 1979, the whole of Bao-an county, which borders Hong Kong, was designated as a "special municipality" with the town of Shenzhen as its centre. This put it on the same political footing as Guangzhou (Canton), the capital of Guangdong province. In March the same status was granted to Zhuhai, the area across the border from Macao. Later in December, the Guangdong provincial government added Shantou (not a border town, but one with a large diaspora, especially in Indonesia and Singapore) to the list of special districts, calling them Special Economic Zones (SEZs) for the first time. In 1980 Fujian province, also given similar permission by the central government, announced the establishment of a Special Economic Zone at Xiamen (Amoy). It was not until 1988 that the fifth and final Special Economic Zone was created. In that year Hainan island was first established as an Special Economic Zone and then hived off from Guangdong province to become a province in its own right. By the time Hainan SEZ was established, the opening-up process had been extended to other areas, as we shall see.

Although they were initially modelled on the export processing zones of East and Southeast Asia, by calling them Special Economic Zones, the Chinese authorities signalled that they would be different — that they would have "Chinese characteristics". The SEZs were not just to be vehicles for expanding exports, they were to have multiple objectives and be "windows and bridges" into the outside world for the Chinese economy and into the Chinese economy for foreigners. Having seen the opportunities and prospects through the "windows", enterprises could then cross the "bridges" provided by the SEZs, in both directions. In addition to being windows and bridges, the SEZs were also to be "economic laboratories" in which economic policy experiments could be tried out on a geographically restricted basis.

The Basic Functions of the SEZs

Windows and Bridges

Trade and foreign investment policy in China came together in the "windows-and-bridges" function of the SEZs. By investing in the SEZs, foreigners could see through the "window" into the Chinese economy; hinterland enterprises investing in the SEZs could see what technology was available and what world market requirements and potentials were for their products. Having seen the benefits, by looking through the windows both ways, these enterprises were expected to use the "bridges" provided by the SEZs to move capital and knowledge into China and move exports of Chinese products, or labour, out of the country. Preferential policies were quickly introduced to stimulate enterprises to look through the windows and to take advantage of the bridges.

The SEZs quickly demonstrated the potential benefits of opening up. They also allowed the fears of the unknown to be quickly overcome, both those of foreigners of conditions in China and those of the Chinese people of the foreigners they had long been taught to regard with suspicion. The combination of the removal on the prohibition of inward foreign investment, the reduction of controls on Chinese enterprises investing in the SEZs and the preferential policies, especially the tax breaks and foreign-exchange retention arrangements, resulted in a surge of economic activity in the SEZs, which was to continue unabated. Foreign and domestic capital flowed into the zones continuously, including in 1989, the year of the Tiananmen Square tragedy. Two-way trade between the SEZs and world markets has grown without a break, as has trade between the SEZs and the hinterland provinces.

The benefits of market forces perceived through the windows of the SEZs and which travelled over the bridges into the hinterland were quickly recognised. More and more areas of China were opened up as windows and bridges, but always on a more restricted basis than in the SEZs. First 14 coastal cities, from Dalian in the north to Beihai in the south, were opened up and then the Yangtze and Pearl river deltas, the Southern Fujian Triangle (Xiamen-Zhangzhou-Quangzhou), and the Liaodong and Jiaodong peninsulas were added to the open areas. In 1990 the Pudong district of Shanghai was established as a special economic-development area with a policy package similar to those being obtained in the SEZs. In 1991 and 1992 the areas in Xinjiang, Inner Mongolia, Guangxi and Yunnan on the borders with Russia and other members of the Commonwealth of Independent States (CIS), Pakistan,

Myanmar and Vietnam were opened. In 1993 six major cities along the Yangtze river were classified as open cities.

Within all of these open areas, including the SEZs themselves, the practice of establishing "zones within zones" was adopted. In these sub-zones, special preferential policies over and above those available in the SEZ or other open areas were applied. These sub-zones include: the 14 Economic and Technological Development Zones approved by the State Council (originally only in the Open Coastal Cities but similar zones sponsored by provincial and municipal governments have now been established in many open areas); the Science and Technology Parks found in many open areas (including the SEZ); the 13 Free Trade Areas in Pudong (Waigaochao), Tianjin, Hainan (Jingpan), Dalian, Zhang Jiagang, Guangzhou, Qingdao, Ningbo, Fuzhou, Shantou, Xiamen and Shenzhen (Shantoujiao and Futian), and the export processing zones in Shenzhen and Pudong.

The window-and-bridge function of the SEZs was most important in their early years, before the familiarity of foreigners with the Chinese economy and that of Chinese enterprises with world markets developed. The spread of the opening-up process means that that function is now shared with a growing number of open areas. For the most part, however, the "economic laboratory" function of the SEZs remains one of their unique features. A similar role has, however, been given to the Pudong Development Area in Shanghai about which Deng Xiaoping said in the spring of 1992 that it was a mistake not to have included Shanghai in the original list of SEZs.

Laboratories

The role of SEZs as laboratories in which economic experiments can be carried out is a very important one. It has proved to be a way of overcoming political resistance to the introduction of market reforms into China and a way of testing how some reforms fit into the Chinese political context. For the most part, the experiments, other than opening up and offering of preferential policies, have been concentrated on Shenzhen and Hainan, with minor experiments also being conducted in Xiamen and Pudong. Zhuhai and Shantou were followers rather than leaders in the laboratory role.

The list of experiments tried out in the SEZs is long. The first and most crucial was the opening-up process itself. As we have seen, prior to the economic reforms initiated in 1978 at the Third Plenary Session of the 11th Central Committee of the CCP, the Chinese economy was effectively closed. Foreign investment, in or out, was prohibited and trade was restricted to planned exports needed to finance imports essential for the attainment of planned targets. There was no rational relationship between world prices and Chinese domestic prices of tradable goods and services. The call by Deng Xiaoping and his supporters to open up the economy and allow foreign investment and market-determined trade was a bold one and met with much resistance. To overcome this opposition, it was proposed that the more liberal reforms should be limited to the SEZs, thus making them politically more acceptable. The gains from the experiment were quickly appreciated, however, and more and more areas of the country were quickly opened up.

The initial trials in opening up to trade and foreign investment led to more experiments. It became clear that to take full advantage of the move towards an economy structured more in line with its comparative advantage would require the adoption of the institutions of market economies, albeit in the context of a Communist political system. To Western eyes, the "socialist market economy" of Deng Xiaoping bears little resemblance to a capitalist economy. Compared to the situation prior to China's opening up, however, the reforms are revolutionary.

The reforms that were tried out on an experimental basis in the SEZs fall into two categories: those concerned with the establishment of markets and those concerned with the creation of a regulatory and administrative framework within which the markets operate. The former have been taken further than the latter (which acts as a constraint on the reform process). The extent to which the experiments have been considered successful and carried over into the hinterland economy varies from case to case.

First, experiments with commodity markets, especially for consumer goods, are those that have been taken the furthest. From the beginning, enterprises established in SEZs have been able to make their production decisions relate more to market forces than to planning directives. They can set their prices freely. Imports from abroad and from the hinterland (except for minor quantities of food still subject to rationing) are sold in open markets and are less subject to tax distortions than in the rest of the economy. The limited experiment of allowing market forces to determine prices has been extended to the rest of the economy, including foodstuffs, in the southern coastal provinces and major metropolitan areas. State-owned enterprises in the rest of the economy are, however, still subject to planning constraints on their production decisions. Even in the SEZs, state-owned enterprises and joint ventures are still not operating according to market forces, since they remain largely protected from the consequences of continued loss-making decisions by the government's unwillingness to allow them to go bankrupt. However, the greater openness of the economies of the SEZs means that there is more competition in commodity markets and that prices there are closer to international levels. This liberalisation has been extended since 1992 to the tertiary sector, with foreign investors being allowed to invest in international and domestic trading activities.

Second, producer-goods markets in SEZs are not as open as consumer-goods markets. The market is less well organised and there is less competition. Continued protection of domestic producers of raw materials, intermediate goods and capital goods means that costs to users are artificially high. The consequential losses, from this and other sources, are passed on to domestic users and in many cases have to be covered by subsidies on export markets. One experiment recently introduced in Shenzhen, Xiamen and Pudong has been the establishment of bonded warehouses for producer goods required by firms in those zones. Producer-goods or secondary-goods markets have developed more or less spontaneously in the domestic economy; in some cases branches of the organisations that run these markets have been established in the SEZs and Pudong. On balance, however, experiments in the establishment of markets for producer goods have been limited in effect, both in the SEZs and hinterland. This is because producer goods are still largely supplied by state-owned enterprises, which are reluctant to allow competition to reduce their market share.

Third, a similar situation to that in the producer-goods markets prevails in the factor markets. There have been reform experiments in all three factor markets

— labour, capital and land — mostly in the SEZs. However, while the reforms have moved a long way, they leave these markets far from the practices prevailing in Western economies. The main reforms in the labour market have been the introduction of the contract system, increased mobility, increased independence for enterprises in hiring and firing and in wage determination, and the central provision of social security benefits. Not all experiments have been tried in all SEZs and where they have, it has not always been to the same extent. All of these experiments have subsequently been extended to parts of the hinterland, although not in all cases as liberally as in the SEZs. Despite the experiments, the labour market in the SEZs remains restrictive. There are strict restrictions on legal movements into the SEZs. Movement between firms and contract extensions require official approval, although the freedom of movement of professionals between firms in the SEZs has recently been eased. Contracts are supervised by the Labour Bureaux, which act as mediators in the case of disputes and which also maintain some control over wage and benefit rates.

In the capital market, the first experiment was the introduction of foreign investors, followed by the introduction of foreign banks, the introduction of commercial banking practices in Chinese banks and the establishment of stock companies, stock markets, stock exchanges and futures markets. All of these experiments have been regarded as successful by the government and transferred to the hinterland, although there is only one stock exchange in an SEZ (Shenzhen) and one outside (Shanghai) and only two joint venture banks, the activities of which are so far restricted to SEZs (Xiamen in one case and Shenzhen in the other)[21]. Despite these experiments, however, the dominant source of capital in the SEZs remains the government, both central and local, either directly from tax revenues or through the transfer of the assets of state-owned enterprises. Chinese banks continue to allocate capital according to the dictates of the national plan, and even in their commercial banking they are often subject to irresistible political pressures to extend credit to loss-making state-owned enterprises. Money market facilities are still limited and restrictive.

The economic experiment that has probably been taken the furthest beyond the SEZs is the development of foreign exchange markets. Foreign-funded enterprises in Shenzhen were initially given permission to swap their surpluses and deficits of foreign exchange at prices agreed between themselves. Swap centres such as these were later established in other SEZs and then in other open areas where foreign-funded enterprises were established. More than 90 fully fledged foreign exchange centres have been established throughout China, although they are not yet linked together into a national system. As the market developed its scope increased, from trade in foreign-exchange retention rights amongst foreign-funded enterprises to trade in currency held by those firms, and retention rights held by Chinese-owned enterprises and other legal entities. While the development of these markets is a significant step along the road to convertibility, there is still a long way to go: as we have seen, access to the markets remains restricted to those who have permission to engage in international transactions. There are still extensive controls over capital movements.

Fourth, the market for land is perhaps that which has seen the greatest break with the past. Prior to the reforms, all land was held by the state. This remains true, but the state is now willing to sell land-use leases for up to 70 years, including to foreign-funded enterprises. The lack of secure land-use rights was a major impediment to foreign investors in the early days of the reforms, especially in the real-estate development sector where land was initially rented on a day-to-day basis. The concept of leases was developed in the agricultural sector in order to induce farmers to take on and develop marginal lands. It was then extended much more radically in the SEZs to land needed for real estate and industrial development in order to offer some security to enterprises investing their capital in developments on the land. Initially the fees for leases were negotiated, but with competition for prime land developing over time, auctions have become increasingly common, except on economic-zone developments where fixed negotiated prices still prevail.

A more radical further reform has been introduced in the land-lease market. This is the sale to foreign investors of the right to develop and manage land, including the conclusion of sub-leases with other foreign firms. The first major project based on this arrangement was a 30 km^2 zone at Yangpu in Hainan, although there had been a smaller such scheme for part of the Economic and Technological Development Zone in Tianjin. There was a great deal of political resistance to Yangpu development (which was reminiscent of the reviled treaty ports). As a result, it was held up until Deng Xiaoping called for bold policy initiatives early in 1992.

The market in land leases is not a complete market. Some land is still allocated by directives, sometimes without charges, and restrictions remain on access to the auctions. In addition, the secondary market in leases and on property built on the leased land is still in an embryonic state. The lack of a proper leasehold law has led to conflicts between freeholders and leaseholders and between head lease holders and sub-tenants.

Finally, there have been many other experiments relating to the environment within which the market experiments are set. For example, the development of a centralised social-security system for urban workers in Hainan, the partial sale of state-owned enterprises in Xiamen to foreign entrepreneurs, the instigation of bankruptcy proceedings against firms in Shenzhen and the introduction of disclosure rules and foreign accountancy practices for firms wishing to be listed on the stock exchanges in Shenzhen and Shanghai are all important experiments in the economics of capitalism.

The Characteristics of the SEZs

While the original inspiration for China's SEZs was the export processing zones (EPZs) of East and Southeast Asia, as the former developed they came to have little resemblance to the latter. Their major differences are in size, structure and role.

The SEZs are much larger than the EPZs of East and Southeast Asia. EPZs are generally limited in area to several hectares, while the SEZs range from the 23.4 km^2 of Zhuhai through the 130 km^2 of Xiamen (extended later to 256 km^2 in 1990), 234 km^2 of Shantou, 327.5 km^2 of Shenzhen to the 34 000 km^2 of Hainan.

Second, EPZs are typically run by management companies or boards controlled by central government units. The government units are often in the Prime Minister's office. On the other hand, the SEZs are government units in their own right;

municipal governments in the cases of Zhuhai, Shantou, Xiamen and Shenzhen and provincial government in the case of Hainan. Pudong differs from the SEZs in that it is not a government unit but is governed by the Shanghai municipal government, which is one of the three metropolitan government units controlled by the central government[22]. Shenzhen, Xiamen and Hainan are independent planning areas with a fair degree of autonomy.

The third crucial distinction between SEZs and EPZs relates to their role. The fact that the SEZ authorities are also local governments hints at the first difference in roles: SEZs are responsible for all of the functions of local government, whereas EPZs are not. The SEZ authorities have to balance their SEZ responsibilities with those of providing education, sanitation, security and basic infrastructure services. In the cases of Xiamen and Shantou, the authorities are also responsible for pre-existing state-owned industries established in the protected "closed economy" era, the needs of which have to be balanced with those of the new industries established under the SEZ policy framework.

The EPZs have a single objective while the SEZs have many. Under the "bridge" function the objectives of the SEZs include stimulating inflows of capital, technology, management skill and market information. Foreign and domestic firms are encouraged to use packages of such inflows to produce for both the foreign and domestic markets. The governments of Xiamen, Zhuhai and Shenzhen are also supposed to encourage the integration of the economies of Taiwan, Macao and Hong Kong, respectively, with that of the mainland, while Shantou is supposed to draw on its more widespread diaspora to support its development.

In terms of policy framework, the EPZ policy consists simply of the removal of some of the constraining features of the standard domestic economic policy instruments. For example, tax rates are reduced, import and export licenses and duties are removed or their effect substantially mitigated, constraints on access to foreign exchange and ability to use it are reduced or removed and any planning restrictions on the establishment of industrial enterprises by foreigners are modified or removed. By contrast, the SEZs, in addition to this geographically restricted policy liberalisation, are also expected to carry out the policy experiments we have already discussed. Subject always to approval by the central government, the municipal and provincial governments controlling the SEZs can introduce liberal regulations and local legislation ahead of the national liberalisation programme. Enterprises in the SEZs are freer of controls over their production and management decisions than firms in the hinterland[23].

In conclusion, it is easy for non-economists to be impressed with the physical development of the Special Economic Zones (SEZs) and Pudong Development Area. Leaving economic accounting aside, it is also easy for economists to be impressed with the sheer physical scale of the development of the zones. The small fishing and agricultural community of Shenzhen, which had a population of 40 000, has been transformed in a little over a decade into a bustling international city of well over 1 million inhabitants. It has all the appurtenances of a modern city: international airport, industrial areas, "high tech" zones, high-rise apartment blocks and joint-venture hotels, theme parks and golf courses, mobile phones and pagers, a growing service sector, and vice. Zhuhai is following the same route, although it is on a smaller scale and there is more emphasis on commercial agriculture and tourism.

Xiamen and Shantou were decaying coastal cities when they were established as SEZs, so the impact is more muted, but still physically very impressive with new transport facilities, hotels, industrial areas and roads mushrooming throughout the municipal areas. Hainan started from an even more underdeveloped state, having been neglected in the development process by all preceding governments; it now has the air of a frontier, with high-spirited entrepreneurial immigrants from the mainland, Hong Kong and Taiwan pushing and dragging the province into the late 20th century. The main centres, such as Haikou, Sanya and Yangpu, are permanent building sites with homes, offices, hotels, roads and other infrastructure facilities being built 24 hours a day and seven days a week. Pudong is now being developed at the same rate.

What role have the SEZs played in China's transition to an open market economy? Putting aside their physical achievements, the developmental role of the SEZs should be seen against the overall achievements of China's open-economy reforms over the past 15 years, to which we will turn in the next chapter.

Notes and References

1. See, for example, the World Bank reports (1988, 1989, 1990, 1992 and 1993a, b) for a review of recent policy developments.

2. Measuring China's GDP (or per capita GDP) in US dollars or purchasing power parities (PPPs) poses a major problem for an international comparison of economic development and trade openness. See Lardy (1992) for a detailed discussion of China's national accounts and trade statistics.

3. It was reported that there are currently 16 export commodities subject to command planning and channelled through a few designated national FTCs, while all other export commodities have been liberalised (*People's Daily*, 29 October 1993).

4. See the section on China in "Exchange Arrangements and Exchange Restrictions" published annually by the IMF for a detailed account of the controls on imports and exports.

5. See p. 36 for the description of foreign-funded enterprises.

6. In addition to import tariffs, the Chinese authorities have maintained a variety of non-tariff measures (NTMs) for various reasons. On the import side, they have used several NTMs such as the mandatory import plan, "canalisation of imports" (i.e. imports allowed only through designated FTCs), import licensing and import controls, though these measures are overlapping to a large extent. Similarly, export licensing and export taxes have been used as the main instruments to control exports, as the mandatory planning for exports was abolished in 1991. The latest information available indicates that in 1992, licensing accounted for over 15 per cent and 25 per cent of China's total exports and imports, respectively. See World Bank, 1993a (pp. 63-69) for a detailed analysis of China's NTMs.

7. The tariff collection rate for 1986 was 9.7 per cent in China (See World Bank, 1993a, p. 60).

8. Such rebates are estimated to have been about 7 per cent of total exports in 1988 (Lardy, 1992, p. 50).

9. There are some minor exceptions (i.e. petroleum products and fees from processing trade). See World Bank (1993a, pp. 29-31) for a more detailed account of China's foreign-exchange markets.

10. See, for example, "Income Tax Law on Foreign-Funded Enterprises and Foreign Enterprises and its Instruction" (*Xinhua Yuebao*, No. 4, 1991, pp. 76-81), which provides the definition of foreign-funded enterprises. "Foreign enterprises" here refers to representative offices of foreign firms in China.

11. According to the 1979 Law on Chinese-Foreign Joint Ventures, the establishment of a JV requires foreign partners to contribute to no less than 25 per cent of equity capital. However, this condition is not necessarily met in practice.

12. However, Thoburn *et al.* (1992) argue that since foreign partners such as Hong Kong firms take a substantial interest in the setting up and initial running of the processing and assembly operations, they are a genuine form of foreign investment in China (p. 216).

13. JEs are of minor importance in China, accounting for only 4 per cent of total actual FDI flow in China in 1991.

14. See Khan (1991, Annex 7) for a summary of some of these concessions operated by the Special Economic Zones. See also Bell *et al.* (1993, pp. 38-45).

15. The 14 Open Coastal Cities are Dalian, Qinhuangdao, Tianjin, Yantai, Qingdao, Lianyungang, Nantong, Shanghai, Ningbo, Wenzhou, Fuzhou, Guangzhou, Zhanjiang and Beihai.

16. For domestic firms, access to the retention rights was limited by the firm's ability to raise domestic credit and to get permission to import, both variables being controlled by the government.

17. *Guanxi* means drawing on connections for privileged access to inputs or markets, rather than relying on arms-length market forces. See Wall (1992a) for a discussion of the concept of *guanxi*.

18. Cowley (1991) argues:

    The life blood of a Chinese company is *guanxi* — connections. Penetrating layers of *guanxi* is like peeling an onion: first come connections between people with ancestors from the same province in China; then people from the same clan or village; finally, the family. It does not matter much whether a Chinese businessman is in Hong Kong or New York, he will always operate through *guanxi* (*The Economist*, 16 November 1991, p. 8).

19. See Yang (1992, p. 22) who argues: "The collection of fees is arbitrary and unjustified financial burdens are levied in various localities."

20. See Crane (1990) for a good introduction to the establishment of the Special Economic Zones.

21. Overseas banks with assets in excess of $10 billion can establish branches, subsidiaries, joint ventures or contractual ventures in China as long as they have had an office open there for three years and appoint a Chinese as a senior manager. Several banks have established branches or subsidiaries on this basis, although only two joint ventures are mentioned in the text. These branches and subsidiaries are restricted to foreign-currency business only and mainly deal with foreign-funded enterprises. See *China Daily Business Weekly*, 14-20 February 1993, p. 2.

22. In January 1993, a Pudong New Area Administrative Committee was established along with its parallel Pudong New Area Communist Party Working Committee. The Administrative Committee is a quasi-governmental body set up to run its Area, with a limited degree of independence from its Municipality. See *Shanghai Star* (8 January 1993) for a full description of the new administrative arrangements for Pudong.

23. The enhanced local autonomy enjoyed by the SEZs is, however, subject to careful scrutiny and control by the central government. How far the SEZs can go in their experiments is a function of the national political climate. The reins have been tightened and slackened several times since 1978. For example, Hainan's controversial

proposal for the Yangpu free-trade area was held up for several years until the climate was changed by Deng Xiaoping's call for bolder policy experiments in his Southern China speeches in 1992. After this speech the State Council approved the project. However, Hainan's bold initiative in setting up a stock exchange in response to Deng Xiaoping's speeches was quickly squashed following the personal intervention of Deputy Premier Zhu Rongji. This reflected the State Council's belief that the stock-exchange experiment should be limited to two locations (Shenzhen and Shanghai) for the time being.

Development of China's Legal Framework for Foreign Direct Investment

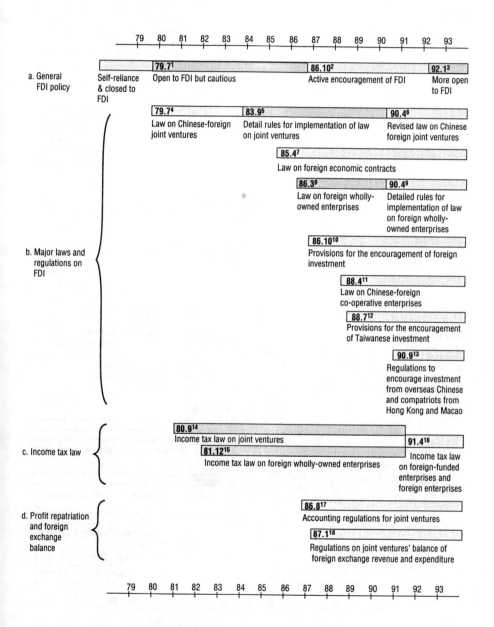

a. General FDI policy

Self-reliance & closed to FDI

79.7¹ Open to FDI but cautious

86.10² Active encouragement of FDI

92.1³ More open to FDI

b. Major laws and regulations on FDI

79.7⁴ Law on Chinese-foreign joint ventures

83.9⁵ Detail rules for implementation of law on joint ventures

90.4⁶ Revised law on Chinese foreign joint ventures

85.4⁷ Law on foreign economic contracts

86.3⁸ Law on foreign wholly-owned enterprises

90.4⁹ Detailed rules for implementation of law on foreign wholly-owned enterprises

86.10¹⁰ Provisions for the encouragement of foreign investment

88.4¹¹ Law on Chinese-foreign co-operative enterprises

88.7¹² Provisions for the encouragement of Taiwanese investment

90.9¹³ Regulations to encourage investment from overseas Chinese and compatriots from Hong Kong and Macao

c. Income tax law

80.9¹⁴ Income tax law on joint ventures

81.12¹⁵ Income tax law on foreign wholly-owned enterprises

91.4¹⁶ Income tax law on foreign-funded enterprises and foreign enterprises

d. Profit repatriation and foreign exchange balance

86.8¹⁷ Accounting regulations for joint ventures

87.1¹⁸ Regulations on joint ventures' balance of foreign exchange revenue and expenditure

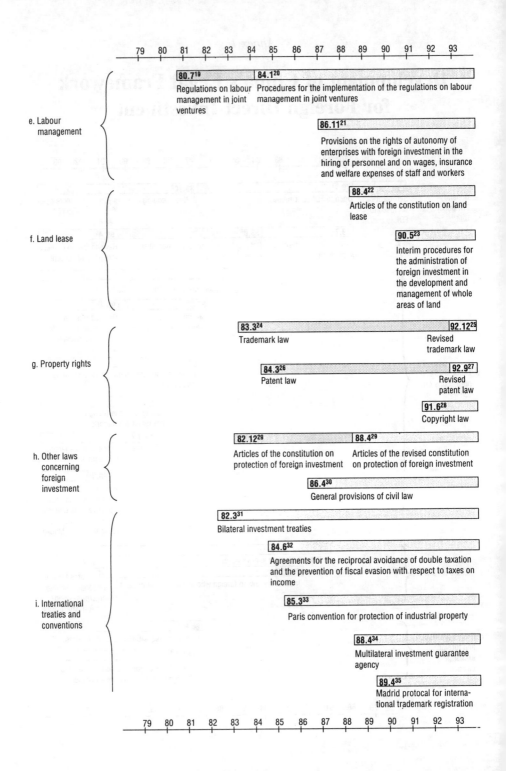

	79	80	81	82	83	84	85	86	87	88	89	90	91	92	93

e. Labour management

80.7[19] Regulations on labour management in joint ventures

84.1[20] Procedures for the implementation of the regulations on labour management in joint ventures

86.11[21] Provisions on the rights of autonomy of enterprises with foreign investment in the hiring of personnel and on wages, insurance and welfare expenses of staff and workers

f. Land lease

88.4[22] Articles of the constitution on land lease

90.5[23] Interim procedures for the administration of foreign investment in the development and management of whole areas of land

g. Property rights

83.3[24] Trademark law

92.12[25] Revised trademark law

84.3[26] Patent law

92.9[27] Revised patent law

91.6[28] Copyright law

h. Other laws concerning foreign investment

82.12[29] Articles of the constitution on protection of foreign investment

88.4[29] Articles of the revised constitution on protection of foreign investment

86.4[30] General provisions of civil law

i. International treaties and conventions

82.3[31] Bilateral investment treaties

84.6[32] Agreements for the reciprocal avoidance of double taxation and the prevention of fiscal evasion with respect to taxes on income

85.3[33] Paris convention for protection of industrial property

88.4[34] Multilateral investment guarantee agency

89.4[35] Madrid protocal for international trademark registration

	79	80	81	82	83	84	85	86	87	88	89	90	91	92	93

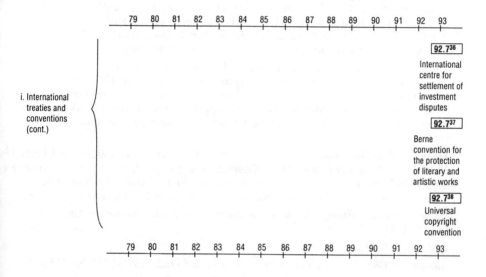

i. International
treaties and
conventions
(cont.)

79 80 81 82 83 84 85 86 87 88 89 90 91 92 93

92.7[36]
International
centre for
settlement of
investment
disputes

92.7[37]
Berne
convention for
the protection
of literary and
artistic works

92.7[38]
Universal
copyright
convention

Notes and References

1. *Guide to China's Foreign Economic Relations and Trade, Investment Special,* Economic Information & Agency, Hong Kong, 1983, pp. 187-189. In July 1979 China promulgated the first Law on Foreign Direct Investment called the Law on Chinese-Foreign Joint Ventures. This marked the very beginning of the Chinese open attitude toward foreign investment. Prior to this law, China adopted a policy to restrain foreign investment and pursue self-reliance economic development.

2. *Guide to China's Foreign Economic Relations and Trade, Investment Special,* 1987-1988, Economic Information and Agency, Hong Kong, pp. 194-196. In October 1986, China promulgated the famous "Twenty Two Articles" to encourage foreign investment with export-oriented and technologically advanced features. This reflected the transition of the Chinese attitude towards FDI from passive waiting to active encouragement.

3. *Xinhua Yuebao* (in Chinese), No. 6, 1992, pp. 39-40 and *People's Daily* (in Chinese) 18 February 1993. It was after Deng Xiaoping gave his speech in South China in early spring 1992 that a real change of attitude towards FDI occurred in China. After that, tertiary sector and on-shore oil exploration were opened for foreign investors.

4. *Guide to China's Foreign Economic Relations and Trade, Investment Special,* 1983, pp. 187-189.

5. *Ibid.,* pp. 189-193.

6. *Almanac of China's Foreign Economic Relations and Trade,* 1991-1992, pp. 113-115.

7. *The China Investment Guide 1986,* pp. 674-678.

8. *Guide to China's Foreign Economic Relations and Trade,* Investment Special, 1987-1988, pp. 210-211.

9. *Almanac of China's Foreign Economic Relations and Trade,* 1991-1992, pp. 123-130.

10. *Guide to Foreign Economic Relations and Trade,* Investment Special, 1987-1988, pp. 194-196.

11. *Almanac of China's Foreign Economic Relations and Trade,* 1989, pp. 102-103.

12. *Ibid.,* 1989, pp. 106-107.

13. *Ibid.,* 1991-1992, pp. 118-119.

14. *Guide to China's Foreign Economic Relations and Trade,* Investment Special, 1983, pp. 246-247.

15. *Ibid.,* pp. 261-263.

16. *Xinhua Yuebao* (in Chinese), No. 4, 1991, pp. 76-78

17. *Almanac of China's Foreign Economic Relations and Trade*, 1988, pp. 209-210.

18. *Ibid.*, 1987, pp. 610.

19. *Guide to China's Foreign Economic Relations and Trade*, 1987-1988, pp. 227-229.

20. *Ibid.*, pp. 249-252.

21. *Ibid.*, pp. 196-197.

22. *Xinhua Yuebao* (in Chinese), No. 4, 1988, p. 37.

23. *Almanac of Foreign Economic Relations and Trade*, 1991-1992, pp. 116-117. Also Lin Shuofu (1990), "On the Development of Whole Areas of Land", *Intertrade Monthly* (in Chinese), No. 12 and Chang Xiuze (1992), "Studies on Issues of the Development of Whole Areas of Land by Foreign Investment in the Mainland", *Economic Studies*, No. 6.

24. Zhen Chengsi (1991), "China's International Property Protection v.s. International Standards, *Intertrade Monthly* (in Chinese), No. 10. pp. 9-12.

25. *People's Daily* (in Chinese), 21 January 1994.

26. Gu Huizhong and Zhou Xiaoqi (1990), "The Establishment and Development of China's Patent System", *Intertrade Monthly* (in Chinese), No. 10.

27. *Xinhua yuebao* (in Chinese), No. 9, 1992, pp. 21-26.

28. Zheng Chengsi (1991), "China's Intellectual Property vs. International Standards", *Intertrade Monthly* (in Chinese), No. 10, and Schloss, Peter A. (1990), "China's Long-Awaited Copyright Law", *The China Business Review*, September-October, pp. 24-28; also see *The China Business Review*, November-December, 1990, p. 5.

29. *Xinhua Yuebao* (in Chinese), No. 4, 1988.

30. *Almanac of China's Foreign Economic Relations and Trade*, 1987, pp. 563-564.

31. *Bilateral Investment Treaties*, 1959-1991, United Nations, New York, 1992, p. 18.

32. *Guide to Foreign Economic Relation and Trade*, Investment Special, 1987-1988, p. 38.

33. Gu Huizhong and Zhou Xiaoqi, *Intertrade Monthly* (in Chinese), No. 10, pp. 9-12, 1990.

34. Shihata, Ibrahim F.I. (1988), *MIGA and Foreign Investment: origins, operations, policies and basic documents of the multilateral investment guarantee agency*, Martinus Nijhoff Publishers, p. 385.

35. Zheng Chengsi (1991), "China Intellectual Property Protection *vs.* International Standards", *Intertrade Monthly* (in Chinese), No. 10.

36. *Xinhua Yuebao* (in Chinese), No. 7, 1992, p. 19.

37. *Ibid.*, p. 19.

38. *Ibid.*, p. 19.

Chapter 3

China as an Emerging Pacific Economy

Introduction

While China is and has always been a regional military power, prior to the 1978 reforms it was basically an underdeveloped agrarian economy, plagued by the devastating consequences of the Great Leap Forward (1958-60) and the Cultural Revolution (1966-76)[1]. Having limited contact with the outside world, the country was lagging far behind neighbouring economies in East Asia.

The economic landscape began to change after the 1978 reforms, though it is important to stress that China did not turn into an outward-oriented economy overnight. The opening-up process has been gradual, and progress uneven. The reform of foreign-exchange policy has been moving far ahead of the reform of commercial policy. Import liberalisation has been much slower than decentralisation of export activity. As for foreign investment, it was not until 1986 that the Chinese authorities switched their policy stance decisively to active encouragement of foreign direct investment (FDI). In a Communist-controlled political regime, the timing and sequencing of open-economy reforms are significantly influenced by internal political developments. A case in point is the creation of SEZs by the Chinese authorities in 1979. This was considered a realistic solution to the politically sensitive question of how "capitalist practices" should be allowed in a Communist political regime, such as China's. The further easing of political constraints led to opening up 14 coastal cities in 1984 and the official announcement of the so-called "coastal development strategy" in 1988. In spite of the temporary setback, both political and economic, in the wake of the Tiananmen Square incident on 4 June 1989, China's pursuit of outward orientation has not changed.

As it enters the 1990s, China has been emerging as a leading Pacific economy with an outstanding economic and trade performance, even amongst the fast-growing developing economies in the Asia-Pacific region. According to some observers, the "Chinese Economic Area" encompassing China, Hong Kong and Taiwan has become a "fourth growth pole" of the world economy, along with the United States, Japan and Europe (Armington and Dadush, 1993). In the present economic downturn facing the OECD countries, the continued rapid growth of China has served as an important countercyclical force for the Asia-Pacific region as a whole, and in particular, East Asian developing economies.

In examining the impact of China's open-economy reforms, it is necessary to see the Chinese experience in the context of the Asia-Pacific region as a whole. Despite the apparently partial nature of its open-economy reforms, China's opening-up policy has provided a sufficiently large market opportunity to attract foreign direct investment from the neighbouring economies of the region, once China moves decisively to outward orientation while getting macroeconomic fundamentals and its exchange-rate policy right. The developmental role of SEZs should also be evaluated in this context.

Perspectives on China's Foreign Trade

Main Developments in China's Merchandise Trade

Overview

The period since 1979 has seen a spectacular growth of China's merchandise exports (Figure III-1). This remarkable export performance has been made possible as the highly centralised trade regime gradually evolved into a more diffused and decentralised one. An increasing number of local enterprises have thus become engaged in foreign-trade activities independently of the trade plan set out by the central government. Prior to the 1978 reforms, the volume of China's merchandise exports was primarily a function of the amount of goods available for exports, which was determined as the "residual" between domestic consumption and production. Although various experiments were undertaken to decentralise the foreign trade regime, the central government had kept it under control until 1984-85. Since then the pace of decentralisation at the provincial and municipal levels has gathered momentum and the pace of export growth has accelerated[2].

The level of China's merchandise imports, by contrast, has fluctuated widely during the post-reform period, primarily reflecting the government's "stop-go" macroeconomic policies. Bell et al. (1993, pp. 66-69) identify four macroeconomic cycles from 1979 to 1993. The first cycle covered the years from 1979 to 1982, followed by three cycles from 1984 to early 1986, from mid-1986 to late 1988 and from late 1991 to 1993[3]. In each of the first three cycles, a sharp rise in merchandise imports (in 1979/80, 1984/85 and 1987/88) due to strong domestic demand and the concomitant credit expansion exacerbated the balance of payments, which led immediately to an import retrenchment (in 1981, 1986 and 1989) by tightening credit allocations and administrative controls on imports. Khor (1991) argues that China's macroeconomic cycles during the post-reform period did not stem from economic reform in itself but rather from its incompleteness. For transitional economies such as China's, macroeconomic adjustment poses a formidable challenge, and in China an effective means of macroeconomic management has yet to be established[4].

The basic trend underlying China's trade development during the post-reform period is such that the rapid expansion of exports was not fast enough to catch up with import expansion. With minor exceptions in 1982 and 1983, the trade balance

Figure III.1. **Merchandise trade of China, 1979-93**

(Billion dollars)

Merchandise imports

Merchandise exports

Sources: Figures for 1979 are from MOFERT, while figures since 1980 are from China's customs statistics. Figures for 1993 are from *Europe News* (in Chinese) March 13-15, 1994.

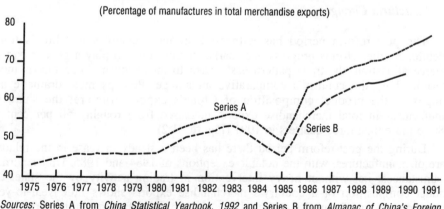

Figure III.2. **China's shift towards exports of manufactures**

(Percentage of manufactures in total merchandise exports)

Series A

Series B

Sources: Series A from *China Statistical Yearbook, 1992* and Series B from *Almanac of China's Foreign Economic Relations and Trade, 1991/1992.*

remained in deficit throughout the 1980s. The combination of the austerity programme introduced in 1989 and the continued strong growth of exports resulted in a sizeable trade surplus in 1990 and it reached nearly $10 billion in 1991. Owing to a domestic consumption boom, however, this surplus dropped to $4.4 billion in 1992. By 1993, China's trade balance had swung back to a *deficit* of $12 billion. Merchandise imports increased by 29 per cent in that year to nearly $104 billion, while merchandise exports were up only 8 per cent to about $92 billion.

Official Chinese trade statistics on the country's bilateral trade differ significantly from those published by some of its major trading partners, particularly the United States[5]. For example, according to China's Customs Statistics, the main source of China's trade surplus in 1991 was a $14.7 billion surplus in trade with Hong Kong, while trade with the United States and the European Community recorded deficits of $1.8 billion and $1.6 billion, respectively. On the other hand, the partners' trade statistics show that in the same year China had trade surpluses of $12.7 billion with the United States and $10 billion with the European Community.

Finger (1992) attempted to reconcile the two sets of trade statistics by redistributing the value of China's indirect exports via Hong Kong according to the partners' import statistics. He showed that in 1990 the estimated share of the Asia-Pacific region in China's total exports was less than 50 per cent, instead of more than 70 per cent reported by China's Customs Statistics. Similarly, Finger estimated the share of China's exports going to North America at 25 per cent and to Western Europe at 19 per cent, compared with the 9 and 10 per cent, respectively, reported by Chinese statistics. Taking into account other possibilities of indirect trade (e.g. through Singapore), it would be safe to say that at least two-thirds of China's exports in 1990 would have been shipped eventually to OECD Member countries. This roughly corresponds to the OECD Member countries' share of total merchandise exports of the Asian NIEs and ASEAN countries.

Structural Change

The post-reform period has witnessed dramatic changes in China's trade structure. As the reforms progress and market forces come to play a greater part in resource allocation, the trade pattern has tended to move towards one that is more determined by the country's comparative advantage. Perhaps most dramatic are changes in the product composition of China's export structure; the share of manufactures in total merchandise exports increased from roughly 50 per cent in 1980 to more than three-quarters in 1991 (Figure III-2).

During the post-reform period there has been a steady increase in the relative share of manufactures, with the notable exceptions of 1984 and 1985. Under normal circumstances, i.e. without heavy intervention in trading activity by the state, the product composition of a country's merchandise exports shows little year-to-year fluctuations. A significant rise in the relative share of manufactures in the early 1980s is largely attributable to the rapid development of "processing and compensation" trade (see below). This is followed by a sharp drop in the relative share of manufactured exports in 1984-85, which corresponds to China's economic boom during which exportables were diverted to domestic consumption. However, such diversion did not occur during the 1988-89 boom period.

It seems that the Chinese experience over the decade from 1985 points to the fact that the trade plans imposed by the central government started to give way to market forces in the mid-1980s. More detailed information on commodity breakdown suggests that China's trade structure has come to display the NIE characteristics, with increased specialisation in exports of labour-intensive products. In 1991 such products as textiles, clothing, footwear, watches and other simple electrical products accounted for at least one third of China's total merchandise exports. At the same time, import substitution of intermediate products (e.g. iron and steel) and capital goods (e.g. vehicles and electrical and industrial machinery) has also made some progress during the same period (Annex 2).

New Forms of Trade

As part of the earlier initiative to encourage foreign investment, the State Council approved alternative forms of trade. Two such forms of trade have become important sources of foreign-exchange earnings for China. These are "processing trade" and "compensation trade". A third form, "barter trade" along China's extensive borders, does not generate foreign-exchange inflows but it has become an important choice and an efficiency-raising economic activity.

Processing trade is based on importing raw materials or intermediate products for conversion into final products in China via the application of labour, plus the use of Chinese infrastructure and land. The final products are all exported. The term covers pure processing trade, such as the conversion of imported cloth into garments, assembly, such as video tapes or umbrellas, and agricultural output such as pigs bred from imported breeding stock or feedstock or cereals based on imported seeds. Foreign investors supply imported inputs under co-operation agreements and pay processing fees to their Chinese partners. On the other hand, *compensation trade* is the practice of foreign investors providing equipment, technology and management support in return for output which is then exported. From small beginnings in 1980 (accounting for only 1 per cent of total merchandise exports), the processing and compensation trades quickly became significant earners of foreign exchange during the early period of economic reform.

The most important location for foreign investment in joint ventures under processing- and compensation-trade agreements is Guangdong province, with the foreign investors coming mainly from Hong Kong. Chinese statistics lump together data for processing trade and compensation trade and it is only available as a separate entry for investment for Guangdong. By the end of 1990, 20 000 ventures were engaged in such activities in Guangdong, employing 1.37 million workers (MOFERT, 1992, p. 324). This compares to 7 079 other forms of foreign-funded enterprise in Guangdong at that time (of which only 810 were listed as Export-Oriented Enterprises and 114 as Technologically Advanced Enterprises). Of the total $11 billion exports from Guangdong in 1990, $661 million, or roughly 6 per cent, were accounted for by processing and compensation trade[6]. This same trade accounted for roughly 7 per cent of the $1.6 billion gross exports of Guangzhou[7]. In

Shenzhen Special Economic Zone (SEZ), the figure was $175 million (about 6 per cent of its total exports), in Zhuhai SEZ $24 million (about 5 per cent), and $88 million (9 per cent) in Shantou SEZ (MOFERT, 1992, pp. 328-331)[8].

Barter trade with the former USSR was more or less non-existent for many years. With the commencement of economic reforms in the former USSR, however, barter trade expanded rapidly, turning into a boom after the collapse of Soviet Communism. In Heilongjiang province, barter trade with Russia in 1990 amounted to a total of 720 million Swiss francs (the usual unit of account for official barter trade), of which imports were 376 million and exports 344 million (MOFERT, 1992, p. 275). In Xinjiang in 1990, barter trade with Russia totalled 35 million Swiss francs for exports and 35 million Swiss francs for imports (MOFERT, 1992, p. 362).

Initially, barter trade took the form of informal trade in free barter markets, but as itinerant traders from Russia began penetrating further into China, the authorities in Beijing moved to set up special markets for them in 1992. Officially recorded barter trade between Russia and China alone was estimated at $2 billion in 1992, compared with $88 million in 1987. In addition, informal unrecorded trade was estimated to "run into tens of millions of dollars annually" (*Financial Times*, 23 February 1993, p. 3).

China's Comparative Advantage and Export Performance

Table III-1 presents changes in the shares of China and its major Asian competitors in the OECD countries' import market during the 1979-91 period. Table III-2 also provides the same set of data on import shares with respect to manufactured goods, defined as SITC codes 5 to 8[9]. China has managed to increase its relative share of the OECD countries' market significantly during this period. Amongst non-OECD countries, China had become the largest exporter to the OECD Member countries by 1991. This occurred while the market share of the non-OECD country exporters had contracted during the same decade because of weak commodity prices. The increase in China's share is explained by the fact that its export structure has rapidly shifted from primary products to manufactured goods. In 1979, at the onset of China's opening to the outside world, primary products accounted for nearly 60 per cent of total imports from China by the OECD Member countries. By 1991, more than 80 per cent of total imports from China by the OECD Member countries were manufactured goods. As seen in Table III-2, China has become the second largest supplier of manufactured goods from non-OECD countries to the OECD Member countries, next to Taiwan.

Amongst the three major OECD countries/regions, China's presence as an emerging exporter is highest in Japan and lowest in OECD Europe (Annex 3 and 4). Although the rise in China's market share had been rapid in OECD Europe from a very small base over the last ten years, China still accounted for less than 1.5 per cent of total imports in OECD Europe in 1991, compared with 3.5 per cent in North America and 6.1 per cent in Japan. For manufactured goods the import shares were 1.3 per cent in OECD Europe, 4.1 per cent in North America and 7.1 per cent in Japan. China's exports of manufactured goods in the OECD countries' market tend to concentrate on a very narrow range of products, involving textiles and clothing,

Table III-1. Share of China and Other Asian Economies in OECD Countries' Total Import Market, 1979-91

(US$ million and percentage)

	1979	Share	1985	Share	1989	Share	1990	Share	1991	Share
CHINA	6 160	0.5	14 673	1.1	36 394	1.6	44 563	1.7	56 746	2.2
ASEAN (4)	31 241	2.7	35 908	2.6	54 599	2.4	61 964	2.4	69 952	2.7
Indonesia	14 723	1.3	16 916	1.2	18 405	0.8	20 816	0.8	21 867	0.8
Malaysia	8 497	0.7	9 608	0.7	15 504	0.7	17 237	0.7	20 211	0.8
Philippines	4 542	0.4	4 770	0.3	7 272	0.3	7 777	0.3	8 352	0.3
Thailand	3 478	0.3	4 615	0.3	13 418	0.6	16 134	0.6	19 522	0.8
NIEs (4)	38 824	3.4	70 706	5.2	140 320	6.3	141 339	5.5	146 714	5.7
Hong Kong	10 600	0.9	15 752	1.1	24 599	1.1	25 114	1.0	25 555	1.0
South Korea	11 037	1.0	19 640	1.4	46 177	2.1	44 286	1.7	44 760	1.7
Singapore	5 208	0.5	8 880	0.6	19 193	0.9	22 523	0.9	23 213	0.9
Taiwan	11 979	1.0	26 435	1.9	50 350	2.3	49 415	1.9	53 186	2.1
SOUTH ASIA (2)	6 128	0.5	7 933	0.6	13 818	0.6	15 807	0.6	16 364	0.6
India	5 123	0.4	6 407	0.5	10 981	0.5	12 299	0.5	12 578	0.5
Pakistan	1 006	0.1	1 527	0.1	2 838	0.1	3 507	0.1	3 786	0.1
TOTAL NON-OECD	371 840	32.3	402 487	29.3	565 557	25.3	639 117	24.9	653 360	25.2
TOTAL WORLD	1 150 404	100	1 372 265	100	2 231 536	100	2 568 007	100	2 589 189	100

Source: OECD, *Foreign Trade by Commodities* (Series C).

Table III-2. **Share of China and Other Asian Economies in OECD Countries' Import Market in Manufactured Goods, 1979-91**

(US$ million and percentage)

	1979	Share	1985	Share	1989	Share	1990	Share	1991	Share
CHINA	2 561	0.4	6 781	0.8	26 898	1.6	34 179	1.8	46 270	2.4
ASEAN (4)	5 719	0.9	9 532	1.1	25 253	1.5	31 186	1.7	38 352	2.0
Indonesia	585	0.1	1 492	0.2	5 032	0.3	6 081	0.3	7 525	0.4
Malaysia	2 382	0.4	3 453	0.4	7 751	0.5	9 576	0.5	12 555	0.7
Philippines	1 428	0.2	2 511	0.3	4 334	0.3	5 097	0.3	5 582	0.3
Thailand	1 323	0.2	2 076	0.2	8 136	0.5	10 431	0.6	12 690	0.7
NIEs (4)	32 860	5.0	62 542	7.3	128 957	7.9	129 281	6.9	134 837	7.1
Hong Kong	10 058	1.5	15 039	1.7	23 416	1.4	23 997	1.3	24 426	1.3
South Korea	9 635	1.5	17 594	2.0	42 662	2.6	40 981	2.2	41 260	2.2
Singapore	2 801	0.4	5 930	0.7	15 943	1.0	18 697	1.0	20 238	1.1
Taiwan	10 365	1.6	23 979	2.8	46 937	2.9	45 605	2.4	48 913	2.6
SOUTH ASIA (2)	3 801	0.6	4 617	0.5	10 412	0.6	12 139	0.6	12 746	0.7
India	3 103	0.5	3 542	0.4	8 061	0.5	9 156	0.5	9 424	0.5
Pakistan	698	0.1	1 075	0.1	2 351	0.1	2 983	0.2	3 322	0.2
TOTAL NON-OECD	88 738	13.6	111 051	12.9	303 939	18.6	330 181	17.6	357 211	18.7
TOTAL WORLD	654 593	100	859 914	100	1 633 899	100	1 872 837	100	1 906 502	100

Source: See Table III-1.

Table III-3. CMS Analysis of Manufactured Exports from China and Other Asian Economies to the OECD Countries' Market, 1979-90

(Percentages)

Country/Period	Actual Export Growth	CMS Decomposition			
		(1)[a] Standard Growth Effect	(2) Product Growth Effect	(3) Market Growth Effect	(4) Competitive Effect
China					
1979-85	164.8	32.8	-11.9	7.2	136.7
1985-90	403.9	116.1	5.6	-0.6	282.7
Indonesia					
1979-85	155.0	32.8	-24.9	11.9	135.2
1985-90	307.9	116.1	6.3	2.9	182.6
Malaysia					
1979-85	44.9	32.8	-5.6	32.3	-14.5
1985-90	178.4	116.1	10.1	-10.3	62.4
Philippines					
1979-85	75.8	32.8	-0.3	41.7	1.6
1985-90	103.0	116.1	15.3	-18.9	-9.5
Thailand					
1979-85	56.9	32.8	-19.7	11.9	31.9
1985-90	403.9	116.1	9.5	-10.2	288.5
Hong Kong					
1979-85	49.5	32.8	5.8	25.0	-14.0
1985-90	59.6	116.1	16.7	-23.8	-49.4
Korea					
1979-85	82.6	32.8	-0.2	27.6	22.5
1985-90	132.9	116.1	4.8	-16.2	28.0
Singapore					
1979-85	111.7	32.8	17.9	27.3	33.8
1985-90	215.2	116.1	11.6	-20.1	107.6
Taiwan					
1979-85	131.3	32.8	4.3	44.3	50.1
1985-90	90.3	116.1	11.0	-33.2	-3.6
India					
1979-85	14.2	32.8	-17.2	10.7	-12.2
1985-90	158.6	116.1	0.2	-7.4	49.6
Pakistan					
1979-85	53.9	32.8	-23.3	2.8	41.8
1985-90	177.4	116.1	-6.6	-0.4	68.3

a. The growth rates reported in this column are slightly different from what one can calculate from Table III-2 (31.4 and 117.8). This is because Table III-2 includes manufactured goods not specified elsewhere at the SITC 2-digit level.

Note: See text for the methodology of the CMS analysis.
Source: The authors' own calculation based on OECD, Commodity Trade Database.

footwear, travel goods, miscellaneous manufactured articles, some electrical products and chemical products (Annex 5). However, in some product lines China has now achieved significant "market shares" as measured by shares of imports into OECD countries (Annex 6). While China's share of total imports of manufactured goods by OECD countries rose from 0.7 per cent in 1981 to 2.4 per cent in 1991, its share increased substantially with respect to a number of product groups defined at the SITC 2-digit level. Although no product group achieved a 5 per cent share in 1981, product groups with a more than 5 per cent share in 1991 were travel goods (29 per cent), footwear (13 per cent), apparel (12 per cent) and miscellaneous manufactured articles n.e.s. (mainly toys) (8 per cent). Higher import shares were gained by China in North America for these product groups. More than 5 per cent of North American imports was also achieved by telecommunication and sound recording appliances (6 per cent) in 1991.

In order to assess the relative export performance of China in the OECD countries' market, a constant-market-share (CMS) analysis was used to decompose China's export growth into: 1) the standard growth effect (i.e. the growth of total imports of OECD Member countries), 2) the product growth effect (i.e. a country's favourable or unfavourable export concentration on particular product groups), 3) the market growth effect (i.e. a country's favourable or unfavourable export concentration on particular regions of the OECD Member countries), and 4) the competitive effect. The last effect is a residual that reflects the difference between the actual export growth and the hypothetical growth rate that would have been attained if the country in question had maintained its share in each regional market of the OECD Member countries with respect to each product group.

The magnitude of these four effects calculated by the CMS analysis may be influenced by various factors, including: a) the selection of a base year, b) different levels of product and market aggregation, c) the order in which the product and market growth effects are calculated, and d) the difficulty of interpreting the residual term (Leamer and Stern, 1970; Richardson, 1971). Despite these drawbacks, the CMS analysis is a useful tool in identifying the relative export performance of a country with respect to its potential competitors under well-specified conditions.

We have performed a CMS analysis using the *import* data set of the 24 OECD Member countries with respect to 11 Asian exporters, 35 manufactured goods (SITC codes 5 to 8 at the 2-digit level) and 4 regional markets (Japan, Australasia, North America and OECD Europe) for 1979-90 (subdivided into the two periods, 1979-85 and 1985-90). The 11 Asian exporters are China, four ASEAN countries (Indonesia, Malaysia, the Philippines and Thailand), four NIEs (Hong Kong, Korea, Singapore and Taiwan) and two South Asian countries (India and Pakistan). The results of the CMS decomposition are presented in Table III-3.

Table III-3 shows, for example, China's manufactured exports to the OECD Member countries to have increased by 164.8 per cent between 1979 and 1985, as calculated from the import statistics of the OECD Member countries. This actual growth rate is decomposed into: 1) a standard growth effect of 32.8 per cent, that is, the growth rate of total manufactured goods imported by the OECD Member countries from all sources, 2) a product growth effect of -11.9 per cent, 3) a market growth effect of 7.2 per cent, and 4) a competitive effect of 136.7 per cent, which is calculated as a residual. These results indicate that more than four-fifths of the growth of China's manufactured exports to the OECD Member countries in 1979-85 can be attributed to the competitive effect. Similarly, the competitive effect accounted for 70 per cent, by far the greatest part, of China's increase in exports to the OECD Member countries during the 1985-90 period.

Table III-3 also shows that the competitive effect was the dominant factor contributing to the growth of manufactured exports from Indonesia throughout the period concerned, and from Thailand during the 1985-90 period. Furthermore, a significant improvement in the export performance of India, Malaysia and Singapore during the second half of the 1980s was linked to a relative improvement in the competitive effect, whereas the better export performance of the Philippines, Korea and Pakistan was largely due to higher import growth of the OECD countries' market.

By contrast, Hong Kong and Taiwan had relatively poor export performances during the second half of the 1980s, with their actual export growth lagging far behind the overall increase in the OECD countries' imports of manufactured goods, partly because of a negative market effect and partly because of declining export competitiveness. The latter is represented by a significant decline in the competitive effect (Column 4).

In spite of the limitations of the CMS analysis, our results are consistent with the recent studies conducted by Yeats (1991) and Jones, King and Klein (1993) on China's revealed comparative advantage (RCA), and by Ariff and Chye (1992) on a CMS analysis of export performance of ASEAN countries. Yeats (1991) argues that except for several natural resource-based products (particularly chemicals) where China has high RCA index, China and Asian NIEs such as Hong Kong and Taiwan — and India as well — have largely competitive export profiles, with China tending to broaden the export base of labour-intensive products[10]. Our results imply that during the decade of reforms China has managed to increase international competitiveness in the market of the OECD countries with respect to East Asian economies such as Hong Kong and Taiwan[11]. Similarly, it appears that the ASEAN countries, except for the Philippines, have generally improved their export competitiveness in the Asia-Pacific region (Ariff and Chye, 1992).

Links between Trade and FDI: Chinese Perspectives

A key aspect of China's ongoing transition to a market economy is the remarkable supply response to new market opportunities created by its opening-up policy. China has successfully converted its export structure to one that is increasingly determined by comparative advantage and has become a competitive exporter of manufactured goods in the world market. It is not easy, however, to explain how transitional economies, like China's, become competitive in the world market. Since the inception of its reform process, China, which had a very rigid command economy, has been undergoing a transformation into a market economy with increasingly decentralised economic management. This has given local authorities and firms increasing opportunities for making economic decisions on their own initiative. Yet China's sustained economic and export growth over a relatively long period is not satisfactorily explained by a steady improvement in allocative efficiency, since the reform process has been gradual and uneven. In a recent paper, Panagariya (1993) points out that China's economic success owes much to "productivity gains from dynamic forces unleashed by the creation of an investment-friendly environment and the subsequent inflow of foreign capital, entrepreneurship, technology and market links (p. 66)".

As we have seen, the rapid expansion of manufactured exports during the past decade and particularly since the mid-1980s is *not* unique to China. For this reason, the Chinese experience must be examined in the context of the Asia-Pacific region as a whole. An important aspect of industrial adjustment by the economies of this region over the past decade or so is a growth of foreign direct investment (FDI) which, in turn, is related to the export of manufactured products[12].

China and the ASEAN countries have been carrying out structural reforms, albeit to varying degrees, dealing with foreign trade and investment, with particular emphasis on market-oriented, outward-looking development strategies[13]. It is crucial that these unilateral liberalisation measures be accompanied by appropriate macroeconomic and exchange-rate policies for stimulating growth and attracting FDI[14]. In this respect, the exchange-rate realignment during the second half of the 1980s of the Japanese yen, and subsequently of the currencies of Taiwan and Korea, certainly played a central role in stimulating the economies of China and the ASEAN countries (except for the Philippines). Like the earlier practice of the United States and Japan, Asian NIEs have been relocating unskilled labour-intensive industries, in which they are losing their comparative advantage, to neighbouring countries with a greater comparative advantage.

Figure III-3 depicts yearly movements of official dollar exchange rates of the Chinese yuan and its real effective exchange rates (REER), i.e. trade-weighted and inflation-adjusted exchange rates, from 1978 to 1991. Both exchange rates are expressed as indices with 1978 as a base year. The REER index was calculated by using official bilateral exchange rates with 1991 trade (exports plus imports) weights of China's 14 largest trading partners (excluding the former USSR)[15]. Inflation differentials between China and these 14 partners were adjusted by using the consumer price indices[16]. From 1978 until 1983, the real effective exchange rate of the yuan *appreciated* by some 30 per cent before depreciating dramatically in the subsequent years. This reflects a successive devaluation of the yuan against the dollar in 1984-86 and again in 1989-91.

To show changes in price competitiveness between China and its main competitors in East and Southeast Asia, China's real bilateral exchange rates were also calculated (Table III-4). Since the mid-1980s the Chinese yuan has depreciated substantially and rapidly, compared to the currencies of Malaysia, Singapore, Taiwan, Thailand, and to a lesser extent, Hong Kong and Korea. On the other hand, the Chinese yuan has tended to appreciate against the Indonesian rupiah and the Philippine peso. The large real depreciation of the Chinese yuan may reflect a decisive shift in China's development strategy in the mid-1980s in favour of the production of traded goods at the expense of non-traded goods. For example, the Chinese authorities implemented major trade reforms in 1984-85 by starting to liberalise trade and foreign-exchange allocation systems, reducing the extent of the mandatory trade plan, opening up 14 coastal cities, and so on.

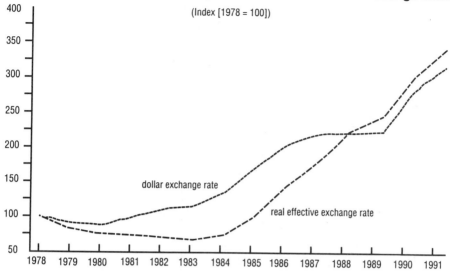

Figure III.3. **China's dollar exchange rates and real effective exchange rates**

(Index [1978 = 100])

dollar exchange rate

real effective exchange rate

Note: See text.

Sources: IMF, *International Financial Statistics,* Direction of Trade. *Statistics and China Statistical Yearbook,* various years.

It has been argued that increasing economic links amongst the economies of the Asia-Pacific region through FDI can be seen as an example of the "flying-geese" pattern of trade development (Chen, 1990; Ozawa, 1990; Yamazawa, 1990; Yamazawa, Hirata and Yokota, 1991). The basic idea of this concept is that the development of Pacific Asian trade involves "catching-up" processes amongst a cluster of economies at different stages of industrialisation and development: the more advanced economies in Pacific Asia (for example, Japan) respond to the advance of the economies immediately following (such as Korea and Taiwan) by moving up the ladder of comparative advantage to exports of more technology or human capital-intensive products, thereby leaving the room for imports of more unskilled labour-intensive, standardised products. Led by the United States and Japan, and followed by Asian NIEs, ASEAN and China, the economies of the Asia-Pacific region are advancing together through trade expansion based on shifting comparative advantage over time[17]. The globalisation of US and Japanese corporate activity through FDI, and more recently, by corporations in Asian NIEs has served as a force that is binding together the economies of this region.

The emergence of a "greater China", comprising China, Hong Kong and Taiwan, may be seen as intrinsic to such "catching-up" processes through the relocation of labour-intensive production activities from Hong Kong and Taiwan to the mainland. The economic linkages between Hong Kong and China, particularly with Guangdong province, that developed during the 1980s have been well documented by Sung (1991) and others[18]. Taiwan has now also become a key player in the evolution of a "greater China". In the following, we review recent trends and

Table III-4. China's Real Bilateral Exchange Rates Based on Consumer Price Index
(1978 = 100)

	1978	1979	1980	1981	1982	1983	1984	1985	1986	1987	1988	1989	1990	1991
Hong Kong	100.0	78.8	71.5	65.3	61.6	49.8	51.5	70.8	86.1	96.0	107.8	115.7	135.8	141.2
Indonesia	100.0	57.4	50.1	51.6	51.0	35.4	34.2	42.8	44.0	36.9	40.2	42.3	48.6	48.4
Korea	100.0	79.5	51.0	43.7	43.1	41.8	47.4	60.7	73.4	89.5	113.4	137.4	154.5	156.6
Malaysia	100.0	96.0	93.8	94.2	99.5	102.8	118.2	157.5	189.1	226.6	256.6	283.8	356.4	386.8
Philippines	100.0	79.9	68.8	67.5	64.1	47.7	25.5	26.3	30.0	33.6	36.3	37.0	37.3	32.0
Singapore	100.0	94.6	91.7	100.2	107.8	114.9	133.8	182.9	235.7	284.5	353.9	419.6	561.7	656.1
Thailand	100.0	85.3	73.6	71.5	73.0	74.9	87.2	104.9	133.9	156.7	185.1	203.4	248.2	271.1
Taiwan	100.0	85.6	74.6	71.2	74.0	77.3	95.1	133.7	187.5	272.1	328.5	398.6	475.3	556.1

Notes: An increase in the RBER index indicates a depreciation of the Chinese yuan against the national currencies of the above economies. The RBER index was calculated by using official exchange rates.

Source: IMF, *IFS*, National statistics.

patterns of foreign direct investment in China and then have a close look at the economic relationship between China and Taiwan.

China's Coastal Strategy and Foreign Direct Investment

An Overview

Attracting foreign direct investment (FDI) has been a main objective of the Chinese authorities as part of their policy reforms in the post-1978 period. Over the past 15 years China has gradually established a legal framework for foreign investors and provided tax and other incentives for them. As seen in Table III-5, the amount of FDI inflow in China was very small from 1979 to 1982. Since 1983, however, China has managed to attract an increasing amount of FDI. Although the ratio of actual FDI to contracted FDI has tended to decline since 1987, when it peaked at 66 per cent, the actual amount of FDI inflow in China averaged over $3 billion a year between 1988 and 1990. This was followed by a surge in FDI which amounted to $4.3 billion in 1991 and $11 billion in 1992. According to the IMF Balance of Payments Statistics, over the past decade China has emerged as the second largest recipient of FDI in absolute terms amongst Asian developing economies, next to Singapore (on the basis of cumulative amount of FDI from 1979 to 1991)[19].

The latest statistics indicate that the contracted amount of FDI inflow in China exceeded $110 billion in 1993, nearly double that of 1992. In 1993 the amount of actual FDI registered a record $25.7 billion, which put the accumulated amount of actual FDI in China since its opening up in 1979 at a level of $60 billion. It should be emphasised, however, that the ratio of actual FDI to contracted (or planned) FDI has declined substantially in the 1990s to around 20 per cent, though it went up slightly in 1993. This is nearly as low as the average ratio which prevailed during the 1979-82 period. Such a marked fall in the utilised FDI ratio in the 1990s may have indicated a deterioration in China's "investment-friendly" environment, and overoptimism on the part of Western investors who were unaware of the continuing difficulties faced by firms investing in China[20].

Trends and Patterns of FDI Inflows

In the process of China's gradual integration into the world economy, overseas Chinese business communities in East and Southeast Asia, including Taiwan, have played a leading role. Hong Kong is the main source of FDI in China. Table III-6 shows that in 1992, 70 per cent of total FDI inflows in China came from Hong Kong and Macao. It should be noted, however, that in China's FDI statistics, investment flows from Hong Kong and Macao include those by subsidiaries of foreign and Chinese firms located there. With the easing of the political tension between the two sides of the Strait, Taiwan has become the second largest source of actual FDI in the mainland, accounting for 9.5 per cent of the total in 1992. Amongst other East and Southeast Asian economies, Singapore is also increasing its presence as a foreign investor in China. With the establishment of the diplomatic relationship between the

Table III-5. **Foreign Direct Investment in China, 1979-93**
(US$ billion and percentage)

Year	Actual FDI (1)	Contracted FDI (2)	Utilisation Rate (1)/(2) %
Cumu.1979-93	60.11	221.37	27.2
Cumu. 1979-82	1.17	6.01	19.4
1983	0.64	1.73	36.7
1984	1.26	2.65	47.5
1985	1.66	5.93	28.0
1986	1.87	2.83	66.1
1987	2.31	3.71	62.4
1988	3.19	5.30	60.3
1989	3.39	5.60	60.6
1990	3.49	6.60	52.9
1991	4.37	11.98	36.5
1992	11.00	58.13	18.9
1993	25.76	110.90	23.2

Sources: *China Statistical Yearbook,* 1993 and *China Economic Digest,* Summer Issue, 1994.

74

Table III-6. **Distribution of Actual FDI by Source** ($US million and percentage)

	1986 Value	1986 Share	1989 Value	1989 Share	1992 Value	1992 Share
Total	1 874.89	100.0	3 392.57	100.0	11 007.51	100.0
OECD Subtotal	709.93	37.9	916.99	27.0	1 594.14	14.5
Japan	201.33	10.7	356.34	10.5	709.83	6.4
United States	314.90	16.8	284.27	8.4	511.05	4.6
Germany	19.28	1.0	81.39	2.4	88.57	0.8
Canada	0.00	0.0	16.95	0.5	58.24	0.5
France	42.30	2.3	4.60	0.1	44.93	0.4
United Kingdom	26.83	1.4	28.48	0.8	38.33	0.3
Australia	60.16	3.2	44.42	1.3	35.03	0.3
Italy	23.17	1.2	30.28	0.9	20.69	0.2
Subtotal of Greater China	n.a.	n.a.	n.a.	n.a.	8 759.57	79.6
HK & Macao	1 132.37	60.4	2 077.59	61.2	7 709.07	70.0
Taiwan	n.a.	n.a.	n.a.	n.a.	1 050.50	9.5
Singapore	13.00	0.7	84.14	2.5	122.31	1.1
Thailand	9.10	0.5	12.68	0.4	83.03	0.8
Philippines	1.08	0.1	1.52	0.0	16.28	0.1
Malaysia	0.41	0.0	0.40	0.0	24.67	0.2
Indonesia	0.49	0.0	1.37	0.0	20.17	0.2
South Korea	n.a.	n.a.	n.a.	n.a.	119.48	1.1

Sources: *China Statistical Yearbook*, various issues, and *Intertrade Monthly* (MOFTEC) No. 4, 1993.

two governments in 1992, Korea is expected to increase FDI in China in the coming years. Actual FDI from Korea amounted to $119 million in 1992. On the other hand, FDI from OECD Member countries has been on the decline, relative to total FDI inflows, from 38 per cent in 1986 to 15 per cent in 1992, although these countries doubled their FDI in China in absolute terms during the same period.

There have been major changes in the sectoral distribution of FDI inflows in China since the mid-1980s. In 1986, contracted FDI in the tertiary sector accounted for as much as 70 per cent of the total FDI, of which the real-estate sector alone attracted 57 per cent. In October 1986, China promulgated the "22 Articles", the aim of which was to promote FDI in export-oriented and high-technology manufacturing industries. In April 1987, the State Planning Commission announced the Regulation on Orientation of Foreign Investment, which identified transportation, communication, energy, metallurgy, construction materials, machinery, chemicals, pharmaceuticals, medical equipment and electronics as "high priority" areas for foreign investment. By 1991, the share of contracted FDI in manufacturing industries, such as textiles, electronics, machinery and chemicals, had increased to 80 per cent of the total FDI.

FDI inflows in China are heavily concentrated in the coastal regions (Table III-7). In 1992, nearly 90 per cent of actual FDI went to 11 provinces and municipalities along the coastal regions, of which Guangdong alone accounted for a third of the total FDI, followed by Jiangsu and Fujian. Certainly, the five Special Economic Zones (SEZs), three in Guangdong, one in Fujian and the whole province of Hainan, and 14 coastal cities have played a significant role in attracting FDI. As of 1991, these SEZs and coastal cities, taken together, accounted for 62 per cent of total FDI flows (actual) in China.

At present, there are four main economic areas competing for FDI. One is the Pearl River delta, including Guangdong and Hainan where about 37 per cent of the total FDI is located (as of 1992). In this area, Hong Kong investors are playing a leading role, together with those from Taiwan, Japan, the United States and Europe. Another area is southern Fujian (Minnan) delta along the Taiwan Strait, where about 13 per cent of the total FDI is located. Taiwanese investors are the leading players in this area. A third area is the Yangtze river delta, which includes Shanghai, Jiangsu, and Zhejiang provinces, which taken together, accounted for about 20 per cent of the total FDI. In this area, investors from Hong Kong, the United States, Europe and Japan are playing a leading role. Finally, a fourth area is located along the Bohai Sea in northern China, including Beijing, Tianjin, Shandong, and Liaoning provinces. This area attracted about 18 per cent of the total FDI. In both Liaoning and Shandong, Japanese and Korean investors are dominant figures because of their geographical proximity, while in Beijing and Tianjin, investors from Hong Kong, Japan, Taiwan, the United States, and Europe play a major role. Such an uneven distribution of FDI is explained partly by the fact that the areas concerned amongst the coastal regions are comparatively well developed, and in part by the geographical proximity and cultural links between these regions and foreign investors. We now turn to the economic relationship between China and Taiwan[21].

Table III-7. **Distribution of Actual FDI by Region in China**
(US$ million and percentage)

Region		1986		1989		1992	
		Value	Share	Value	Share	Value	Share
Nation Total		1 874.89		3 392.57		11 007.51	
Region Total		1 373.17	100.0	3 056.45	100.0	10 723.08	100.0
Guangdong	*	722.68	41.5	1 156.44	37.8	3 551.50	33.1
Fujian	*	61.49	3.5	328.80	10.8	1 416.34	13.2
Jiangsu	*	18.11	1.0	93.58	3.1	1 460.04	13.6
Beijing		139.94	8.0	318.46	10.4	349.85	3.3
Shanghai	*	147.65	8.5	422.12	13.8	481.08	4.5
Shandong	*	19.39	1.1	131.32	4.3	973.35	9.1
Liaoning	*	41.28	2.4	118.57	3.9	489.56	4.6
Hainan	*	**	**	94.97	3.1	452.55	4.2
Zhejiang	*	18.53	1.1	51.81	1.7	232.38	2.2
Tianjin	*	29.31	1.7	28.01	0.9	107.24	1.0
Shaanxi		37.16	2.1	97.19	3.2	45.53	0.4
Guangxi	*	36.95	2.1	45.94	1.5	178.33	1.7
Hubei		12.41	0.7	22.95	0.8	203.08	1.9
Hebei	*	6.85	0.4	26.86	0.9	110.19	1.0
Henan		6.05	0.3	42.66	1.4	52.15	0.5
Sichuan		15.23	0.9	8.01	0.3	101.85	0.9
Helongjiang		17.42	1.0	22.41	0.7	70.50	0.7
Hunan		9.48	0.5	6.43	0.2	128.53	1.2
Jiangxi		4.58	0.3	5.87	0.2	96.53	0.9
Jilin		0.57	0.0	3.35	0.1	65.97	0.6
Anhui		7.94	0.5	4.78	0.2	50.02	0.5
Shanxi		0.15	0.0	8.82	0.3	53.84	0.5
Yunnan		3.54	0.2	7.40	0.2	23.13	0.2
Guizhou		2.20	0.1	7.47	0.2	19.79	0.2
Xinjiang		12.81	0.7	0.88	0.0	0.00	0.0
Inner Mongolia		0.98	0.1	0.24	0.0	5.20	0.0
Gansu		0.42	0.0	1.11	0.0	0.35	0.0
Ningxia		0.05	0.0	0.00	0.0	3.52	0.0
Qinghai		0.00	0.0	0.00	0.0	0.68	0.0
Subtotal of coastal regions		1 102.24	63.3	2 498.42	81.74	9 452.56	88.15

Notes: * are coastal provinces and municipalities.

** included in figure for Guangdong province.

Sources: *China Statistical Yearbook*, various issues, and *Intertrade Monthly* (MOFTEC), No. 4, 1993.

China-Taiwan Economic Relations

In July 1992 Taiwan enacted a bill to lift a longstanding ban on a wide range of contacts with China, including visits by Chinese Communist Party members and direct air and shipping links[22]. Since 1949, Taiwan had followed a policy of "Three Nos" ("no contact", "no negotiation", "no compromise"), which was modified in 1985 to "no direct trade", "no official contact" and "no interference with indirect trade". Thus Taiwan's move in July 1992 marked an important turning point in relations between Taiwan and China. The change in Taiwan's official stance is bound to have important repercussions on the economic climate of the region. As will be seen below, there has been a dramatic rise in trade and investment flows across the Straits through Hong Kong in recent years.

Figure III-4 shows "two-way" trade development of China and Taiwan via Hong Kong from 1979 through 1991. The value of indirect trade between China and Taiwan increased from less than $80 million in 1979 to over $1 billion in 1985, and then quadrupled between 1987 and 1990 to reach more than $4 billion. In 1991, there was a further 43 per cent increase to $5.8 billion. Except for the initial years, the balance of this bilateral trade has been in Taiwan's favour.

During the same 1979-91 period, there have also been major changes in the structure of indirect trade between China and Taiwan. Table III-8 presents a breakdown by products of manufactured exports from China to Taiwan via Hong Kong at the SITC 2-digit level, while Table III-9 presents a similar breakdown of manufactured exports from Taiwan to China via Hong Kong. Both tables were

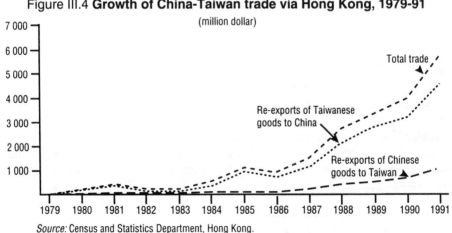

Figure III.4 **Growth of China-Taiwan trade via Hong Kong, 1979-91**

Source: Census and Statistics Department, Hong Kong.

compiled from trade data provided by the Census and Statistics Department of Hong Kong.

While Taiwan's indirect exports to China are predominantly manufactured goods throughout the period, China's indirect exports to Taiwan have displayed a significant shift from primary products (mainly, ores and minerals and food products) to manufactured goods such as textiles (SITC 65) and clothing (84), electrical machinery and equipment (77) and chemical products (5). At the same time, Taiwan's indirect exports to China have become much more diversified. In 1979, textiles alone accounted for more than four-fifths of total indirect exports from Taiwan to China. By 1991, the share of textiles had dropped to less than 40 per cent. On the other hand, chemical fibres (58), industrial machinery (72) and electrical machinery and equipment (77) have emerged as top export items from Taiwan to China through Hong Kong. These changes in the structure of indirect trade between China and Taiwan during the past decade reflect growing economic links across the Strait through FDI.

It is quite difficult to determine the precise evolution of Taiwanese FDI in China, due to a paucity of data and shortcomings in the data available. Nonetheless, it is reasonably estimated that FDI from Taiwan grew rapidly — from $100 million in 1987 to $1 billion in 1992 (Table III-6). Taiwan has become one of the four largest investors in China, together with Hong Kong, Japan and the United States[23]. The surge in Taiwanese FDI in China via Hong Kong has been fuelled by several distinct factors involving both Taiwan and the world economy. Taiwan's firms have been facing growing competition from other NIEs in Asia and the Pacific, due to rising domestic labour costs and the real appreciation of its currency. The export competitiveness of Taiwanese firms has been further eroded by rising operation costs of firms renting plants and factories, because of a real-estate boom that developed after the relaxation of foreign-exchange controls in July 1987. In addition, it has become increasingly difficult for Taiwan's firms to enlarge their market share in the OECD countries' market, in part because of import quotas imposed under voluntary export restraints (VERs) and other market-sharing arrangements.

Small and medium-sized enterprises (SMEs) are the first amongst those affected by these developments. According to Hsiao and So (1992), SMEs viewed the government's policies encouraging industrial restructuring, diversification of trade and relocation of labour-intensive industries to Southeast Asia as, at best, a long-term solution to Taiwan's development, and as an ineffective remedy for their own survival. They were thus the first to engage in "unofficial" trade with the mainland in order to take advantage of the availability of abundant low-wage workers. The change in government policy in 1985 enabled them to begin visiting the mainland, initially to assess the economic environment and later to strengthen their family and social ties with mainland Chinese. This has helped Taiwan's SMEs bypass bureaucratic red tape and unnecessary fees. In addition, they have formed many "self-reliant mutual aid associations" along territorial or industrial lines, to protect themselves and their properties (Hsiao and So, 1992).

Taiwanese FDI received another boost in July 1988, when China promulgated Regulations on Encouraging the Investment of Taiwanese[24]. In October 1989, Taiwan introduced further regulations concerning indirect trade, investment and technical co-operation with the mainland, which led to a skyrocketing of contracted direct

Table III-8. Re-exports of Chinese Goods to Taiwan via Hong Kong
($US thousand and percentage)

SITC CODE	1979	Share	1985	Share	1989	Share	1990	Share	1991	Share
5	2 239	4.0	11 918	10.3	70 771	12.1	71 574	9.4	97 985	8.7
51	818	1.5	2 537	2.2	18 131	3.1	17 050	2.2	27 764	2.5
52	115	0.2	3 439	3.0	22 617	3.9	20 811	2.7	26 048	2.3
53	27	0.0	583	0.5	6 920	1.2	6 625	0.9	13 762	1.2
54	1 131	2.0	3 262	2.8	8 344	1.4	11 107	1.5	11 995	1.1
55	26	0.0	121	0.1	2 825	0.5	3 493	0.5	4 084	0.4
56					13	0.0	42	0.0	110	0.0
57					38	0.0	39	0.0	9	0.0
58			10	0.0	2 540	0.4	4 256	0.6	4 336	0.4
59	121	0.2	1 967	1.7	9 343	1.6	8 150	1.1	9 877	0.9
6	555	1.0	14 701	12.7	126 265	21.5	169 856	22.2	247 611	22.0
61	209	0.4	235	0.2	9 767	1.7	25 590	3.3	19 826	1.8
62			1	0.0	36	0.0	168	0.0	525	0.0
63			13	0.0	3 982	0.7	6 202	0.8	7 489	0.7
64	28	0.1	103	0.1	2 126	0.4	4 254	0.6	5 016	0.4
65	311	0.6	11 980	10.3	67 437	11.5	69 009	9.0	134 794	12.0
66	3	0.0	155	0.1	8 449	1.4	14 586	1.9	17 325	1.5
67			2	0.0	14 570	2.5	11 172	1.5	27 691	2.5
68			2 023	1.7	13 052	2.2	29 994	3.9	19 081	1.7
69	4	0.0	188	0.2	6 846	1.2	8 882	1.2	15 863	1.4

Table III-8 (continued)

SITC CODE	1979	Share	1985	Share	1989	Share	1990	Share	1991	Share
7	77	0.1	103	0.1	57 067	9.7	102 093	13.3	163 671	14.5
71					8 211	1.4	13 274	1.7	13 604	1.2
72			2	0.0	2 340	0.4	3 209	0.4	4 513	0.4
73					991	0.2	2 057	0.3	2 744	0.2
74			2	0.0	3 291	0.6	6 813	0.9	9 520	0.8
75			20	0.0	10 502	1.8	14 257	1.9	12 987	1.2
76	1	0.0	3	0.0	10 516	1.8	14 164	1.9	33 260	3.0
77	1	0.0	73	0.1	20 477	3.5	45 389	5.9	82 426	7.3
78	38	0.1	2	0.0	734	0.1	2 927	0.4	4 617	0.4
79					6	0.0	3	0.0	0	0.0
8	575	1.0	718	0.6	81 844	13.9	143 374	18.7	255 876	22.7
81			0	0.0	678	0.1	1 786	0.2	3 726	0.3
82	555	1.0	49	0.0	5 726	1.0	6 405	0.8	8 706	0.8
83			2	0.0	3 629	0.6	6 365	0.8	12 699	1.1
84			14	0.0	36 942	6.3	75 825	9.9	124 194	11.0
85			26	0.0	2 169	0.4	4 262	0.6	5 967	0.5
86										
87			22	0.0	882	0.2	1 907	0.2	3 087	0.3
88			3	0.0	1 397	0.2	5 524	0.7	31 887	2.8
89	21	0.0	603	0.5	30 421	5.2	41 719	5.5	65 609	5.8
Manufactures Total	3 446	6.1	27 440	23.7	335 947	57.2	486 897	63.6	765 142	68.0
Total Trade	56 284	100	115 901	100	586 901	100	765 357	100	1 125 942	100

Source: Census and Statistics Department, Hong Kong.

Table III-9. **Re-exports of Taiwanese Goods to China via Hong Kong**
($US thousand and percentage)

SITC CODE	1979	Share	1985	Share	1989	Share	1990	Share	1991	Share
5	737	3.4	22 413	2.3	325 866	11.3	414 720	12.7	678 077	14.5
51	472	2.2	434	0.0	25 741	0.9	33 467	1.0	47 634	1.0
52	27	0.1	1 819	0.2	7 114	0.2	6 354	0.2	11 844	0.3
53	0	0.0	528	0.1	11 457	0.4	17 847	0.5	31 467	0.7
54			340	0.0	738	0.0	1 444	0.0	2 737	0.1
55			1 101	0.1	1 093	0.0	3 322	0.1	4 168	0.1
56			21	0.0	672	0.0	173	0.0	141	0.0
57			0		0		0		90	0.0
58	233	1.1	16 111	1.6	257 141	8.9	320 819	9.8	533 143	11.4
59	6	0.0	2 060	0.2	21 909	0.8	31 293	1.0	46 856	1.0
6	18 527	86.3	530 206	53.7	1 337 790	46.2	1 717 580	52.4	2 399 914	51.4
61	146	0.7	6 235	0.6	150 893	5.2	167 454	5.1	234 743	5.0
62	1	0.0	381	0.0	4 857	0.2	5 722	0.2	10 524	0.2
63	472	2.2	9 075	0.9	26 867	0.9	37 032	1.1	40 673	0.9
64	98	0.5	14 771	1.5	43 313	1.5	74 342	2.3	134 576	2.9
65	17 491	81.4	426 280	43.2	981 311	33.9	1 296 837	39.6	1 776 251	38.1
66	19	0.1	5 280	0.5	14 273	0.5	14 699	0.4	18 979	0.4
67	266	1.2	17 581	1.8	27 229	0.9	21 984	0.7	29 614	0.6
68	0	0.0	39 309	4.0	39 155	1.4	43 160	1.3	76 575	1.6
69	34	0.2	11 296	1.1	49 893	1.7	56 351	1.7	77 982	1.7

Table III-9. (continued)

SITC CODE	1979	Share	1985	Share	1989	Share	1990	Share	1991	Share
7	2 011	9.4	342 566	34.7	951 095	32.8	796 709	24.3	1 084 905	23.2
72	635	3.0	81 511	8.3	325 039	11.2	202 743	6.2	279 978	6.0
73	336	1.6	20 194	2.0	51 513	1.8	39 201	1.2	61 941	1.3
74	71	0.3	16 735	1.7	62 526	2.2	57 249	1.7	78 556	1.7
75	4	0.0	22 498	2.3	30 338	1.0	29 673	0.9	54 457	1.2
76			46 084	4.7	132 473	4.6	154 452	4.7	161 534	3.5
77	207	1.0	142 479	14.4	268 565	9.3	222 237	6.8	286 326	6.1
78	41	0.2	6 244	0.6	46 969	1.6	59 832	1.8	124 872	2.7
79					285	0.0	142	0.0	3	0.0
8	75	0.3	75 621	7.7	180 690	6.2	238 202	7.3	343 858	7.4
81			2 115	0.2	6 873	0.2	11 566	0.4	14 918	0.3
82	0	0.0	1 481	0.2	2 089	0.1	2 546	0.1	3 997	0.1
83			396	0.0	4 816	0.2	5 087	0.2	7 030	0.2
84	1	0.0	1 251	0.1	5 944	0.2	6 469	0.2	10 976	0.2
85			6 708	0.7	1 283	0.0	1 095	0.0	3 165	0.1
86										
87			2 405	0.2	11 124	0.4	16 467	0.5	21 709	0.5
88			13 280	1.3	16 601	0.6	24 722	0.8	54 502	1.2
89	73	0.3	47 986	4.9	131 960	4.6	170 250	5.2	227 560	4.9
Total Manufactures	21 350	99.4	970 807	98.4	2 795 440	96.5	3 167 210	96.6	4 506 754	96.6
Total Trade	21 475	100	986 837	100	2 896 487	100	3 278 255	100	4 667 160	100

Source: Census and Statistics Department, Hong Kong.

investment with Taiwan's firms. More recently, the Taiwanese authorities have been trying to guide FDI flows to the mainland rather than to curb them. In September 1990, the Ministry of Economic Affairs requested spontaneous registration and reporting of previous investment in China by April 1991, and authorised over 3 000 products for indirect investment; in general, labour-intensive industries that are no longer competitive in Taiwan are allowed to invest indirectly in the mainland (Chiu and Chung, 1992).

Data on Taiwanese FDI in China shows the following general characteristics[25]. First of all, Taiwanese FDI is similar to that of Hong Kong. It is characterised by OEM arrangements and a heavy concentration in labour-intensive industries such as footwear, electric and electronic components, plastic products and clothing. Investment projects are typically small-scale, reflecting the underlying structure of the Taiwanese economy, in which SMEs account for more than 70 per cent of Taiwan's manufactured exports, and also the entrepreneurial spirit of SMEs compared to the larger firms[26]. According to one observer, Taiwanese FDI projects are relatively small and short-lived, geared to reaping quick profits:

> Taiwan businessmen's investment at the early stages consisted mainly of small entities of several hundred thousands of US dollars. . . Owing to their small sizes, and to the incentive measures of the mainland, a large number of the entities made profits in the same year when the agreement of the investment was executed (Li, 1992, p. 5).

A large proportion of Taiwanese investment is in export processing and export industries. Chiu and Chung (1992, p. 12) note:

> It is reported that 70-80 per cent of Taiwan invested factories export 100 per cent of their products and they rely heavily on the supply of materials and parts from Taiwan. . . One can easily match the 20 fastest rising export commodities with the top 20 invested industries.

These export items are mainly intermediate inputs used in such industries as textiles and clothing, consumer electronics and footwear. However, they also note that exports and FDI rankings are not necessarily in the same order. Two industries in particular, electric and electronic components and vehicles, have accumulated the highest FDI flows but have shown less reliance on material supplies from Taiwan.

Another interesting characteristic is the relationship between FDI and indirect exports of machinery from Taiwan. This has been attributed to the fact that many of Taiwan's investors send depreciated or spare machinery and equipment to their subsidiaries in the mainland. For example, 67 per cent of the electronics industry is reported to have utilised used machinery from Taiwanese investors, though some firms combine new and old machinery (Chiu and Chung, 1992, p. 14).

In terms of regional distribution, Taiwanese FDI is heavily concentrated in Fujian and Guangdong provinces due mainly to their geographical proximity and cultural affinities. However, FDI in Jiangsu province is also substantial[27], and there is information that some Taiwan investors are gradually expanding to other coastal cities and even the interior provinces[28]. These investors are probably attracted by natural resources and even lower labour costs than in the mainland's southern provinces.

Developmental Role of the SEZs

For the Chinese accustomed to the slower pace of development in other parts of the country or for foreigners accustomed to the slower pace of development, if any, in other developing countries, the visual impact of the Special Economic Zones (SEZs) is overwhelming. In particular, it contrasts with the situation in the former Soviet Union and its former satellite states. The sense of awe inspired by the physical development of the SEZs is enhanced by the gross figures tracking the development of the economies of the zones. In the fastest growing SEZ, Shenzhen, the GNP grew from 0.27 billion yuan in 1980 to 17.4 billion yuan in 1991. In the slowest growing, Xiamen, the GNP grew from 0.64 billion yuan to 6.2 billion yuan during the same period. Capital investment in the five SEZs in 1991 amounted to 16.9 billion yuan, of which 6.7 billion yuan was in Shenzhen. Also by the end of 1991, roughly 6 200 industrial enterprises (excluding village enterprises) were established in the five SEZs. Of these, about 1,900 were set up in Shenzhen. In 1991, exports from the five SEZs amounted to $9.5 billion, approximately one-sixth of China's total exports, compared with just over $200 million and roughly 1 per cent of China's total exports in 1981. Of total exports from the five SEZs in 1991, Shenzhen SEZ alone accounted for almost 60 per cent, with a total of $5.6 billion, and foreign-funded enterprises in Shenzhen SEZ contributed to more than half of its 1991 exports (Wall, 1993b)[29].

These growth rates of GNP and exports are phenomenal by international standards. However, economists are a dismal lot and tend to ask awkward questions about the opportunity costs of the resources used to support such development. In a country with the size of China, if resources are collected throughout the country by governments, banks and enterprises and invested in four or five relatively small locations, then it should not be too surprising if the physical impact is dramatic. Indeed, most of the physical investment in the SEZs is of hinterland and local governments, domestic banks and state-owned enterprises. If it has been attracted to the zones by higher rates of return that the investment can earn there, then there is a *prima facie* case that the investment is an efficient use of China's resources. If, however, those rates of return are high because of distortions introduced into the markets by government interventions, then the investment may not lead to an increase in efficiency on a national basis.

The fact is that much of domestic investment in the SEZs has been attracted by policy measures that have artificially raised the rate of return to capital invested there. In the first place, there are substantial tax breaks for Chinese enterprises investing in the SEZs either on their own account or even more as a partner in a joint venture. Second, there is easier access to duty-free imports, free of most controls. Until recently all firms in the SEZs could also retain a larger share of their foreign-exchange earnings (which could be sold at a premium), although this differential incentive has now been removed. Third, firms in the SEZs are freer of planning controls than firms elsewhere, and they are able to take entrepreneurial production and marketing decisions aimed at raising profits rather than simply seeking to meet plan targets. This investment can be suspected of not being efficient in *national* terms. This suspicion receives some support from the fact that, as in the hinterland, about one-third of all Chinese firms in the zones are recognised to be loss-making when using Chinese accounting conventions. By Western accounting standards the ratio is probably much higher.

Doubts can also be raised about the quality of much of the investment in the SEZs. Much of the domestic investment has been made in highly protected import-substitution industries, such as assembly of electronic equipment and video tapes. Some of the joint-venture investment is also oriented towards the domestic market and can only survive because of protection. This will present problems when China rejoins the GATT. Moreover, much of the phenomenal growth in manufactured exports simply involves the export of labour used in "low-technology" industries. The bulk of the investment by overseas Chinese from Hong Kong, Taiwan and elsewhere is in low-value-added, labour-intensive activities. The range includes garments produced under processing agreements, toys and plastic goods, umbrellas, shoes, radios and telephones. More "high-technology" products are now being produced, such as fax machines, computers and disk drives, and video recorders, but the processes used to produce them are labour-intensive and mostly in the form of standardised assembly. Some of the investors seek quick payback investment that only survives during tax holidays, and some are simply fly-by-night operators who disappear when difficulties arise.

Some foreign investors take advantage of the poorly developed auditing and regulatory facilities in China and are engaged in fraudulent transfers of income out of the country, reporting losses for tax purposes when in fact the firm is profitable. For example, a careful audit of ten foreign-funded enterprises in Xiamen that had reported losses uncovered the fact that seven of them were in fact profit-making. There is also considerable scope for collusion with corrupt officials, which can and does stimulate social unrest. Of course, low-quality investment also exists away from the SEZs, and spreads as more and more localities compete to attract investment, especially in the mushrooming Economic and Technological Development Zones, but the freer environment in the SEZs means that the problems tend to loom largest there[30].

Suggestions that the net economic return to China from the investment in the SEZs might not be as great as it seems at first glance usually lead to the reaction that the assessment is based on too narrow a focus. The Chinese authorities recognise that much investment in the zones is of the "low-technology" nature and superficial and that many exports have a high import content. Corruption and vice are also a serious problem; to some extent, this is accepted on the grounds that you cannot have an "open-door" policy without having some mosquitoes fly through, and that it is an inevitable concomitant of setting up the SEZs for their "window-and-bridge" roles. Attention is drawn to efforts being made to control and reduce the impact of these problems, and is also drawn to the other role of the SEZs: that of being "economic laboratories".

Once the merits of the economic experiments tried out in the SEZs have been demonstrated and accepted, many of them have been transferred to the hinterland with beneficial effects in terms of improved economic efficiency. As indicated above, there are many examples of such experiments. Possibly the most important factor in the opening-up process, after the acceptance of any foreign investment at all, was the establishment of markets for foreign exchange. The introduction of competitive bidding for construction contracts with foreign firms, the establishment of a contract system for labour in industry, the establishment of a leasehold system for land and an auction system for selling leases, the introduction of stock companies and stock exchanges, and the introduction of centralised social security systems are several examples of many important economic experiments that were first tried out in the SEZs and later extended to the hinterland, partially or nationally.

There is no doubt that the experience gained from the experiments carried out in the SEZs and the economic benefits from their transfer to the hinterland have made an important contribution to economic reform and economic development in China as a whole. It is, however, difficult to quantify the actual benefits of the experiments in such a way that they could be incorporated into a cost-benefit analysis[31]. Apart from the economic calculations in terms of allocative efficiency, the general perception of the "successes" of the experiments in the SEZs has strengthened the political position of those who are in favour of economic reform and opening up. This has helped ensure the continuation and strengthening of China's open-economy reforms.

Notes and References

1. Prior to the 1978 reforms, the agriculture sector accounted for about 70 per cent of China's total labour force (China Statistical Yearbook, 1992).

2. According to the World Bank (1992), the annual rate of growth of China's merchandise exports (at 1987 constant prices) is estimated at 17.1 per cent per annum during the 1985-91 period compared to 10.4 per cent during the 1980-85 period.

3. See also Khor (1991) and Bell and Kochhar (1992).

4. See Asian Development Bank (1993) and Rana and Dowling (1993) for a detailed discussion of macroeconomic versus microeconomic reforms in transitional economies in Asia.

5. Large discrepancies in bilateral-trade figures originate from differences in the reporting system with respect to rules of origin and destination. Harding (1992, p. 20) states:

   > US statistics consider Chinese goods shipped through Hong Kong to be Chinese exports, but count American goods trans-shipped through Hong Kong as exports to Hong Kong, rather than as exports to China. Chinese statistics, in contrast, include most imports from the United States but consider Chinese goods trans-shipped through Hong Kong as exports to Hong Kong, rather than as sales to the United States.

6. The share of foreign-exchange inflows by processing and compensation trade is, in fact, much higher than this figure suggests, because only actual net payment of foreign exchange for China's value added is recorded in these types of trade, while other types of export figures are recorded "gross" of import content.

7. This accounts for about 2 per cent of the city's total GNP.

8. It should be noted that all MOFERT trade data for the Special Economic Zones include entrepot trade for the hinterland.

9. This definition of "manufactures" understates the relative importance of manufactures in China's total exports, because it excludes processed food products which are important export items for China — about 12 per cent in 1990. For the same reason, the relative importance of manufactures is also understated in Table III-2 with respect to the ASEAN countries.

10. See Annex 2.

11. The results of CMS analysis by Chai (1989, p. 160) reported a negative "competitive effect" during the period of 1982-87, which led him to conclude:

> . . . despite a decade of reforms, China has yet to establish a trade system which would enable it to compete successfully with its East Asian counterparts in the world market for finished manufactures.

However, the results of his CMS analysis were misleading, because in his study, manufactured exports from China (SITC 7 and 8 only) were taken from China's Customs Statistics — not from its partners' import statistics. This procedure not only excluded the bulk of manufactured goods, semi-finished and finished (SITC 5 and 6) from his sample, but also distorted the distribution of China's manufactured exports by destination, as we discussed above.

12. See, for example, Riedel (1991) for the recent trend in intraregional FDI amongst Pacific Asian economies.

13. See, for example, Lardy (1992), Wall (1992a) and World Bank (1992 and 1993a) for China, and Fukasaku, Lee and O'Connor (1993) for six DAEs (Dynamic Asian Economies — Hong Kong, Korea, Malaysia, Singapore, Taiwan and Thailand).

14. It is worth noting that uninterrupted inflows of commercial funds in these Asian economies are in sharp contrast with the problem of liquidity shortage facing many developing countries in other areas.

15. These 14 trading partners are Hong Kong, Japan, the United States, Germany, Korea, Singapore, Italy, France, Canada, Australia, Indonesia, the United Kingdom, the Netherlands and Malaysia. China's trade with these 14 partners accounted for 82 per cent of its total merchandise trade in 1991.

16. The REER index was also calculated by using GDP deflators but the basic trend of the two series is quite similar.

17. See Fukasaku (1992a) for empirical evidence of the so-called, "flying-geese" pattern of trade development.

18. According to one report, there are at present some 25,000 firms operating in Guangdong, with 3 million Chinese employees. About two-thirds of these Chinese employees are engaged in outward processing activities. Two-way investment between Hong Kong and China has been increasing rapidly: Hong Kong's investment in China has now amounted to over $10 billion, while China's investment in Hong Kong has surpassed $12 billion. About four-fifths of Hong Kong's investment in China is directed to Guangdong province (Baldinger, 1992, p. 14).

19. See p. 36 of Chapter 2 for the definition of China's FDI statistics.

20. The decline in the utilised FDI ratio may also reflect in part a longer time-lag involved in foreign-investment projects as the average amount of FDI per project tends to get larger.

21. In order to understand better the trade-FDI links in East Asia, it is important to examine in some detail the evolution of the economic relationship between China and Taiwan, two longstanding political adversaries.

22. "Taiwan Passes Bill Easing China Curbs", *International Herald Tribune*, 17 July 1992.

23. The Taiwanese authorities have recently put in practice compulsory registration of Taiwanese investment in the mainland. This showed that the total amount reached $3 billion (*Europe News*, in Chinese, 16 June 1993).

24. In July 1988, Beijing announced that Taiwanese investors could put money into any project on the mainland, as compared with foreigners, who were limited to industries targeted for development. It also promised to speed their investment application process, and guaranteed that there would be no nationalisation of Taiwanese-owned

assets and that secrecy would be maintained (*Financial Times*, 7 July 1988, as cited in Hartland-Thunberg, 1990, p. 121).

25. See Chung (1992), Chiu and Chung (1992) and Li (1992).

26. Chiu and Chung (1992) note in a comparison of Taiwanese FDI in ASEAN countries and China that the average investment on the mainland ($930 thousand) is far below that in the ASEAN countries ($4.54 million).

27. See *Europe News* (in Chinese) 4 December 1993.

28. See, for example, Pomfret (1992) in the case of Taiwanese investment in Jiangsu province.

29. According to the latest information available at the time of writing, in 1992 exports from the four mainland SEZs and the 14 Open Coastal Cities amounted to $8.5 billion (10 per cent of China's total exports) and $15.1 billion (17.8 per cent), respectively (*Statistical Survey of China, 1993*). However, the relative importance of the SEZs and Open Coastal Cities in China's exports may be overstated because of "entrepôt" trade involved in the statistics (see also note 8 above).

30. The State Council has decided to restrict the proliferation of "zones" (*International Herald Tribune*, 8 February 1993).

31. See Lin (1991) and Chen (1993) for an application of cost-benefit analysis to the SEZs.

Annex 2. China's Merchandise Trade by Product, 1985 and 1991
(Percentage)
A. Merchandise Exports

Category	1985	1991
Primary Products	*50.6*	*22.5*
Food	13.9	10.0
Beverages and Tobacco	0.4	0.7
Raw Materials	9.7	4.8
Fuels	26.1	6.7
Animal and Vegetable Oils	0.5	0.2
Manufactures	*49.4*	*77.5*
Chemicals	5.0	5.3
Manufactured Goods Classified Chiefly by Material	16.4	20.1
of which:		
Textiles	11.9	10.8
Non-metal Mineral Products	0.8	2.3
Metal Products	1.6	2.4
Machinery and Transport Equipment	2.8	9.9
of which:		
Power Machinery and Equipment	0.2	0.5
Specialised Industrial Machinery	0.6	0.8
Telecommunications, Receiving and Recording Equipment	0.3	2.8
Electrical Power Machinery, Appliances and Parts	0.4	2.3
Miscellaneous Products	12.7	23.1
of which:		
Clothing	7.5	12.5
Footwear	0.9	3.2
Cameras, Optical Goods and Watches	0.2	0.9
Products n.e.s.	12.5	19.0

a.   Product category is based on SITC Rev.1 at the two-digit level.

b.   "Products n.e.s." is largely related to processing and assembly trade, and thus included in "Manufactures".

Source: China Statistical Yearbook, 1992.

(Percentage)

B. Merchandise Imports

Category	1985	1991
Primary Products	*12.5*	*17.0*
Food	3.7	4.4
Beverages and Tobacco	0.5	0.3
Raw Materials	7.7	7.8
Fuels	0.4	3.3
Animal and Vegetable Oils	0.3	1.1
Manufactures	*87.5*	*83.0*
Chemicals	10.6	14.5
of which:		
Manufactured Fertiliser	3.6	5.1
Artificial Resin, etc.	3.4	3.7
Manufactured Goods Classified Chiefly by Material	28.2	16.4
of which:		
Textiles	3.8	5.8
Iron and Steel	16.9	4.2
Non-ferrous Metals	3.9	1.3
Machinery and Transport Equipment	38.4	30.7
of which:		
Specialised Industrial Machinery	12.0	9.3
Office Machines and Automatic Data Processing Equipment	2.5	1.4
Telecommunications, Receiving and Recording Equipment	6.0	3.3
Electrical Power Machinery, Appliances and Parts	3.1	4.1
Land Vehicles	7.6	2.9
Miscellaneous Products	4.5	3.8
of which:		
Scientific Instruments etc	2.1	1.4
Cameras, Optical Goods and Watches	0.9	0.7
Products n.e.s.	5.8	17.5

Notes and Sources: See previous page.

Annex 3. Share of OECD Countries' Total Imports by Region

(US$ million and percentage of world total)

OECD

	1981	1985	1989	1990	1991
World	1 306 081	1 372 264	2 231 536	2 568 007	2 589 189
	100	100	100	100	100
OECD	840 433	960 392	1 645 925	1 903 375	1 911 745
	64.35	69.99	73.76	74.12	73.84
Non-OECD	463 004	402 483	565 557	639 117	653 360
	35.45	29.33	25.34	24.89	25.23
China	10 879	14 673	36 394	44 563	56 746
	0.83	1.07	1.63	1.74	2.19

Japan

	1981	1985	1989	1990	1991
World	140 830	127 512	207 356	231 223	234 103
	100	100	100	100	100
OECD	47 762	49 748	102 615	114 871	113 313
	33.91	39.01	49.49	49.68	48.40
Non-OECD	93 061	77 762	104 737	116 348	120 788
	66.08	60.98	50.51	50.32	51.60
China	5 292	6 483	11 146	12 053	14 216
	3.76	5.08	5.38	5.21	6.07

North America

	1981	1985	1989	1990	1991
World	336 114	434 763	604 880	631 783	624 962
	100	100	100	100	100
OECD	197 619	295 325	394 242	405 101	398 837
	58.80	67.93	65.18	64.12	63.82
Non-OECD	138 412	139 401	209 197	225 224	224 058
	41.18	32.06	34.58	35.65	35.85
China	2 246	4 518	13 838	17 455	21 903
	0.67	1.04	2.29	2.76	3.50

OECD Europe

	1981	1985	1989	1990	1991
World	799 698	780 270	1 370 246	1 657 071	1 683 725
	100	100	100	100	100
OECD	573 891	592 052	1 111 358	1 346 255	1 364 732
	71.76	75.88	81.11	81.24	81.05
Non-OECD	223 543	179 230	240 336	286 845	297 043
	27.95	22.97	17.54	17.31	17.64
China	2 968	3 333	10 356	13 905	19 124
	0.37	0.43	0.76	0.84	1.14

Source: OECD, *Foreign Trade by Commodities.*

Annex 4. Share of OECD Countries' Manufactured Imports by Region

(US$ million and percentage of world total)

OECD

	1981	1985	1989	1990	1991
World	698 909	858 270	1 633 899	1 872 837	1 906 502
	100	100	100	100	100
OECD	595 739	716 636	1 314 266	1 521 803	1 530 187
	85.24	83.50	80.44	81.26	80.26
Non-OECD	101 871	139 966	303 939	330 181	357 211
	14.58	16.31	18.60	17.63	18.74
China	4 593	6 781	26 898	34 179	46 270
	0.66	0.79	1.65	1.82	2.43

Japan

	1981	1985	1989	1990	1991
World	30 330	35 792	98 279	109 828	112 948
	100	100	100	100	100
OECD	19 865	23 746	58 707	70 437	68 311
	65.50	66.34	59.73	64.13	60.48
Non-OECD	10 465	12 046	39 572	39 391	44 636
	34.50	33.65	40.26	35.87	39.52
China	1 246	1 567	5 536	5 886	8 017
	4.11	4.38	5.63	5.36	7.10

North America

	1981	1985	1989	1990	1991
World	197 313	320 725	472 982	480 575	486 530
	100	100	100	100	100
OECD	152 597	242 731	332 280	335 278	333 119
	77.34	75.68	70.25	69.77	68.47
Non-OECD	44 678	77 989	139 953	144 540	152 265
	22.64	24.32	29.59	30.08	31.30
China	1 385	3 032	12 259	15 631	20 150
	0.70	0.95	2.59	3.25	4.14

OECD Europe

	1981	1985	1989	1990	1991
World	449 224	478 524	1 022 017	1 242 760	1 268 478
	100	100	100	100	100
OECD	404 402	430 400	890 122	1 080 261	1 097 754
	90.02	89.94	87.09	86.92	86.54
Non-OECD	43 840	46 783	116 967	139 461	152 811
	9.76	9.78	11.44	11.22	12.05
China	1 704	1 924	8 151	11 634	16 714
	0.38	0.40	0.80	0.94	1.32

Source: OECD, *Foreign Trade by Commodities.*

Annex 5a. Profiles of OECD Countries' Manufactured Imports from China by Product

(1981 — US$ million and percentage)

SITC		OECD		North America		Japan		OECD Europe	
5-8		4,593	100	1,385	100	1,246	100	1,704	100
5	Chemicals and related products, n.e.s.	705	15.34	140	10.08	228	18.33	308	18.08
51	Organic chemicals	212	4.62	26	1.91	79	6.30	101	5.92
52	Inorganic chemicals	160	3.48	40	2.89	60	4.83	53	3.12
53	Dyeing, tanning and colouring materials	8	0.18	1	0.07	3	0.22	4	0.25
54	Medical and pharmaceutical products	81	1.76	22	1.57	14	1.16	41	2.43
55	Essential oils and perfume materials	48	1.05	12	0.89	6	0.45	29	1.72
56	Fertilisers other than group 272	1	0.01		0.00	1	0.05	0	0.00
57	Plastics in primary forms	56	1.21	28	2.00	7	0.59	19	1.09
58	Plastics in non-primary forms	14	0.31	0	0.00	7	0.59	5	0.32
59	Chemical materials and products, n.e.s.	125	2.73	10	0.75	51	4.13	55	3.22
6	Manufactured goods classified chiefly by material	1,858	40.45	464	33.47	607	48.71	662	38.84
61	Leather, leather manufactures and dressed furskins	59	1.28	3	0.20	19	1.50	37	2.18
62	Rubber manufactures, n.e.s.	4	0.09	1	0.05	0	0.01	3	0.18
63	Cork and wood manufactures (excl. furniture)	23	0.51	7	0.48	6	0.45	10	0.60
64	Paper and paper manufactures	19	0.42	3	0.21	4	0.31	11	0.66
65	Textile yarn, fabrics and related products	1,182	25.72	308	22.20	306	24.57	460	26.99
66	Non-metallic mineral manufactures, n.e.s.	139	3.03	39	2.81	58	4.62	36	2.13
67	Iron and steel	173	3.77	7	0.54	159	12.73	7	0.41
68	Non-ferrous metals	120	2.60	45	3.22	51	4.06	22	1.28
69	Manufactures of metal, n.e.s.	138	3.01	52	3.74	6	0.46	75	4.41

Annex 5b. **Profiles of OECD Countries' Manufactured Imports from China by Product**

(1981 — US$ million and percentage)

SITC	OECD		North America		Japan		OECD Europe	
7 Machinery and transport equipment	119	2.59	46	3.34	38	3.04	26	1.55
71 Power generating machinery and equipment	9	0.20	2	0.14	0	0.01	6	0.34
72 Specialised machinery	1	0.03	0	0.04	0	0.03	0	0.02
73 Metal working machinery	12	0.27	6	0.44	1	0.05	3	0.20
74 Other industrial machinery and parts	39	0.86	31	2.21	0	0.04	7	0.42
75 Office machines and ADP equipment	1	0.02	0	0.00	0	0.00	1	0.06
76 Telecommunications and sound recording apparatus	8	0.17	4	0.25	1	0.07	2	0.15
77 Electrical machinery, apparatus and appliances, n.e.s.	11	0.23	3	0.21	2	0.16	3	0.20
78 Road vehicles	3	0.06	0	0.04	0	0.01	2	0.11
79 Other transport equipment	35	0.75	0	0.02	33	2.67	1	0.06
8 Miscellaneous manufactures articles	1 912	41.62	736	53.10	373	29.92	708	41.53
81 Prefabricated buildings, sanitary, heating and lighting fixtures	4	0.09	1	0.08	0	0.03	2	0.14
82 Furniture and parts thereof	101	2.19	20	1.42	39	3.15	35	2.08
83 Travel goods, handbags, etc.	42	0.91	17	1.21	2	0.15	22	1.26
84 Articles of apparel and clothing accessories	1 197	26.06	507	36.59	250	20.08	384	22.52
85 Footwear	141	3.07	44	3.16	21	1.72	61	3.57
87 Professional and scientific instruments, n.e.s.	10	0.21	1	0.09	0	0.03	8	0.45
88 Photo apparatus, optical goods, watches and clocks	15	0.32	2	0.18	0	0.02	11	0.65
89 Miscellaneous manufactured articles, n.e.s.	403	8.76	144	10.38	59	4.74	185	10.86

Annex 5c. Profiles of OECD Countries' Manufactured Imports from China by Product

(1991 — US$ million and percentage)

SITC		OECD		North America		Japan		OECD Europe	
		46 270	100	20 150	100	8 017	100	16 714	100
5	Chemicals and related products, n.e.s.	2 088	4.51	447	2.22	634	7.91	950	5.68
51	Organic chemicals	553	1.20	98	0.49	150	1.87	289	1.73
52	Inorganic chemicals	584	1.26	105	0.52	257	3.21	204	1.22
53	Dyeing, tanning and colouring materials	77	0.17	29	0.15	8	0.10	37	0.22
54	Medical and pharmaceutical products	357	0.77	90	0.45	62	0.77	199	1.19
55	Essential oils and perfume materials	91	0.20	29	0.14	20	0.25	38	0.22
56	Fertilisers other than group 272	13	0.03	0	0.00	9	0.11	0	0.00
57	Plastics in primary forms	65	0.14	11	0.06	24	0.30	30	0.18
58	Plastics in non-primary forms	13	0.03	3	0.02	3	0.04	6	0.04
59	Chemical materials and products, n.e.s.	335	0.72	81	0.40	101	1.26	148	0.88
6	Manufactured goods classified chiefly by material	6 938	14.99	2 099	10.42	2 042	25.47	2 508	15.00
61	Leather, leather manufactures and dressed furskins	99	0.21	13	0.06	12	0.15	73	0.44
62	Rubber manufactures, n.e.s.	34	0.07	13	0.07	2	0.03	13	0.08
63	Cork and wood manufactures (excluding furniture)	303	0.66	74	0.37	102	1.27	120	0.72
64	Paper and paper manufactures	181	0.39	80	0.39	22	0.28	67	0.40
65	Textile yarn, fabrics and related products	3 241	7.00	902	4.48	993	12.39	1 186	7.10
66	Non-metallic mineral manufactures, n.e.s.	799	1.73	285	1.41	154	1.92	313	1.87
67	Iron and steel	644	1.39	94	0.47	491	6.12	54	0.33
68	Non-ferrous metals	262	0.57	82	0.41	143	1.78	37	0.22
69	Manufactures of metal, n.e.s.	1 375	2.97	556	2.76	123	1.54	643	3.85

Annex 5d. **Profiles of OECD Countries' Manufactured Imports from China by Product**

(1991 — US$ million and percentage)

SITC		OECD		North America		Japan		OECD Europe	
Machinery and transport equipment	7	7 166	15.49	3 668	18.20	725	9.05	2 579	15.43
Power generating machinery and equipment	71	306	0.66	87	0.43	111	1.38	106	0.64
Specialised machinery	72	87	0.19	42	0.21	15	0.19	26	0.15
Metal working machinery	73	123	0.27	32	0.16	10	0.13	77	0.46
Other industrial machinery and parts	74	648	1.40	370	1.84	47	0.59	201	1.20
Office machines and ADP equipment	75	568	1.23	314	1.56	56	0.70	191	1.14
Telecommunications and sound recording apparatus	76	3 094	6.69	1 664	8.26	189	2.36	1 178	7.05
Electrical machinery, apparatus and appliances, n.e.s.	77	1 907	4.12	1 003	4.98	272	3.40	566	3.39
Road vehicles	78	370	0.80	130	0.64	18	0.23	205	1.23
Other transport equipment	79	63	0.14	27	0.13	6	0.08	28	0.17
Miscellaneous manufactures articles	8	30 078	65.01	13 936	69.16	4 616	57.57	10 677	63.88
Prefabricated buildings, sanitary, heating and lighting fixtures	81	351	0.76	199	0.99	10	0.12	128	0.77
Furniture and parts thereof	82	590	1.28	274	1.36	98	1.22	191	1.15
Travel goods, handbags, etc.	83	2 384	5.15	1 078	5.35	208	2.60	1 015	6.07
Articles of apparel and clothing accessories	84	12 928	27.94	4 447	22.07	3 252	40.57	4 814	28.80
Footwear	85	3 867	8.36	2 779	13.79	313	3.91	683	4.09
Professional and scientific instruments, n.e.s.	87	240	0.52	111	0.55	18	0.23	107	0.64
Photo apparatus, optical goods, watches and clocks	88	764	1.65	311	1.54	84	1.04	358	2.14
Miscellaneous manufactured articles, n.e.s.	89	8 954	19.35	4 736	23.51	632	7.89	3 381	20.23

Source: OECD, *Foreign Trade by Commodities.*

Annex 6a. Profiles of OECD Countries' Manufactured Imports from World Total and China by Products

(1981 — US$ million and percentage)

SITC		OECD			North America			Japan			OECD Europe		
		Total	China	Share	Total	China	Share	Total	China	Share	Total	China	Share
5-8		698 898	4 593	0.66	197 313	1 385	0.70	30 330	1 246	4.11	449 224	1 704	0.38
5	Chemicals & related products, n.e.s.	88 138	705	0.80	13 310	140	1.05	6 200	228	3.68	66 024	308	0.47
51	Organic chemicals	24 882	212	0.85	3 750	26	0.70	1 847	79	4.25	18 648	101	0.54
52	Inorganic chemicals	12 373	160	1.29	2 564	40	1.56	1 015	60	5.93	8 441	53	0.63
53	Dyeing, tanning & colouring materials	4 603	8	0.18	608	1	0.15	281	3	0.99	3 587	4	0.12
54	Medical & pharmaceutical products	9 142	81	0.88	1 297	22	1.68	1 150	14	1.26	6 442	41	0.64
55	Essential oils & perfume materials	4 418	48	1.09	572	12	2.15	203	6	2.76	3 513	29	0.84
56	Fertilisers other than group 272	4 624	1	0.01	1 331	0	0.00	252	1	0.23	2 922	0	0.00
57-9	Chemical materials & products, n.e.s.	28 085	195	0.69	3 188	38	1.19	1 451	66	4.55	22 471	79	0.35
6	Manufactured goods classified chiefly by material	187 916	1 858	0.99	47 633	464	0.97	9 502	607	6.39	125 766	662	0.53
61	Leather, leather manufactures & dressed furskins	4 124	59	1.43	734	3	0.39	157	19	11.93	3 181	37	1.17
62	Rubber manufactures, n.e.s.	8 185	4	0.05	2 120	1	0.04	179	0	0.04	5 548	3	0.06
63	Cork & wood manufactures (excl. furniture)	6 207	23	0.38	1 609	7	0.41	168	6	3.36	4 308	10	0.24
64	Paper & paper manufactures	20 083	19	0.10	4 596	3	0.06	479	4	0.82	14 358	11	0.08
65	Textile yarn, fabrics & related products	31 779	1 182	3.72	1 434	308	21.44	1 704	306	17.96	24 063	460	1.91
66	Non-metallic mineral manufactures, n.e.s.	24 636	139	0.57	5 991	39	0.65	1 127	58	5.11	16 981	36	0.21
67	Iron & steel	39 768	173	0.44	14 132	7	0.05	1 067	159	14.87	23 692	7	0.03
68	Non-ferrous metals	30 465	120	0.39	7 834	45	0.57	4 085	51	1.24	18 337	22	0.12
69	Manufactures of metal, n.e.s.	22 663	138	0.61	6 111	52	0.85	535	6	1.06	15 299	75	0.49

Annex 6b. Profiles of OECD Countries' Manufactured Imports from World Total and China by Product
(1981 — US$ million and percentage)

SITC		OECD			North America			Japan			OECD Europe		
		Total	China	Share	Total	China	Share	Total	China	Share	Total	China	Share
Machinery & transport equipment	7	302 402	119	0.04	103 147	46	0.04	8 815	38	0.43	179 278	26	0.01
Power generating machinery & equipment	71	22 218	9	0.04	7 571	2	0.02	627	0	0.03	13 223	6	0.04
Specialised machinery	72	30 436	1	0.00	9 665	0	0.01	812	0	0.05	18 207	0	0.00
Metal working machinery	73	8 988	12	0.14	3 083	6	0.20	297	1	0.19	5 328	3	0.06
Other industrial machinery & parts	74	33 464	39	0.12	7 701	31	0.40	1 007	0	0.05	23 292	7	0.03
Office machines & ADP equipment	75	25 277	1	0.00	6 047	0	0.00	1 053	0	0.00	17 254	1	0.01
Telecom. & sound recording apparatus	76	25 944	8	0.03	10 653	4	0.03	460	1	0.18	14 021	2	0.02
Electrical machinery, apparatus & appliances, n.e.s.	77	40 694	11	0.03	11 779	3	0.03	1 848	2	0.11	25 852	3	0.01
Road vehicles	78	91 608	3	0.00	30 785	0	0.00	493	0	0.02	46 936	2	0.00
Other transport equipment	79	23 774	35	0.15	5 064	0	0.01	2 218	33	1.50	15 156	1	0.01
Miscellaneous manufactures articles	8	120 441	1 912	1.59	33 223	736	2.21	5 814	373	6.41	78 155	708	0.91
Prefabricated buildings, sanitary, heating & lighting fixtures	81	2 075	4	0.19	335	1	0.35	26	0	1.21	1 667	2	0.14
Furniture & parts thereof	82	8 318	101	1.21	1 666	20	1.18	244	39	16.12	6 273	35	0.57
Travel goods, handbags, etc.	83	2 504	42	1.66	945	17	1.77	174	2	1.11	1 303	22	1.65
Articles of apparel & clothing accessories	84	33 504	1 197	3.57	8 962	507	5.65	1 813	250	13.80	22 299	384	1.72
Footwear	85	9 437	141	1.50	3 536	44	1.24	307	21	6.99	5 435	61	1.12
Profes. & scientific instruments, n.e.s.	87	14 473	10	0.07	2 948	1	0.04	979	0	0.04	9 979	8	0.08
Photo apparatus, optical goods, watches & clocks	88	14 399	15	0.10	4 084	2	0.06	761	0	0.02	9 057	11	0.12
Miscellaneous manufactured articles, n.e.s.	89	35 731	403	1.13	10 746	144	1.34	1 510	59	3.91	22 141	185	0.84

Annex 6c. **Profiles of OECD Countries' Manufactured Imports from World Total and China by Products**

(1991 — US$ million and percentage)

SITC	Product	OECD Total	OECD China	OECD Share	North America Total	North America China	North America Share	Japan Total	Japan China	Japan Share	OECD Europe Total	OECD Europe China	OECD Europe Share
5-8		1 906 502	46 270	2.43	486 530	20 150	4.14	112 948	8 017	7.10	1 268 478	16 714	1.32
5	Chemicals & related products, n.e.s.	224 436	2 088	0.93	33 432	447	1.34	16 864	634	3.76	169 501	950	0.56
51	Organic chemicals	55 569	553	1.00	10 008	98	0.98	4 979	150	3.01	39 779	289	0.73
52	Inorganic chemicals	19 511	584	2.99	4 131	105	2.54	2 674	257	9.62	12 353	204	1.65
53	Dyeing, tanning & colouring materials	13 981	77	0.55	2 057	29	1.43	715	8	1.08	10 967	37	0.34
54	Medical & pharmaceutical products	31 506	357	1.13	4 104	90	2.20	3 114	62	1.99	23 301	199	0.85
55	Essential oils & perfume materials	15 410	91	0.59	2 112	29	1.36	865	20	2.36	12 076	38	0.31
56	Fertilisers other than group 272	6 982	13	0.19	1 255	0	0.01	432	9	2.03	5 029	0	0.00
57-9	Chemical materials & products, n.e.s.	81 477	414	1.48	9 765	95	2.71	4 086	128	6.91	65 996	183	0.85
6	Manufactured goods classified chiefly by material	400 382	6 938	1.73	75 144	2 099	2.79	30 254	2 042	6.75	287 766	2 508	0.87
61	Leather, leather manufactures & dressed furskins	6 571	99	1.50	990	13	1.28	257	12	4.68	5 220	73	1.39
62	Rubber manufactures, n.e.s.	20 475	34	0.17	4 895	13	0.27	816	2	0.28	14 134	13	0.10
63	Cork & wood manufactures (excl. furnitures)	14 609	303	2.08	2 539	74	2.92	1 743	102	5.83	10 136	120	1.19
64	Paper & paper manufactures	52 563	181	0.34	10 187	80	0.78	1 182	22	1.90	40 023	67	0.17
65	Textile yarn, fabrics & related products	67 830	3 241	4.78	9 769	902	9.23	4 327	993	22.94	51 879	1 186	2.29
66	Non-metallic minerals manufactures, n.e.s.	57 641	799	1.39	11 990	285	2.38	4 830	154	3.18	39 969	313	0.78
67	Iron & steel	68 568	644	0.94	12 237	94	0.77	5 470	491	8.97	50 010	54	0.11
68	Non-ferrous metals	55 400	262	0.47	10 149	82	0.81	9 462	143	1.51	35 383	37	0.10
69	Manufactures of metal, n.e.s.	56 726	1 375	2.42	12 389	556	4.49	2 166	123	5.69	41 011	643	1.57

Annex 6d. Profiles of OECD Countries' Manufactured Imports from World Total and China by Product

(1991 — US$ million and percentage)

SITC		OECD			North America			Japan			OECD Europe	
		Total	China	Share	Total	China	Share	Total	China	Share	Total	China	Share
Machinery & transport equipment	7	908 244	7 166	0.79	276 315	3 668	1.33	37 573	725	1.93	574 455	2 579	0.45
Power generating machinery & equipment	71	57 955	306	0.53	19 768	87	0.44	2 068	111	5.36	34 967	106	0.30
Specialised machinery	72	68 104	87	0.13	15 291	42	0.28	2 832	15	0.54	48 167	26	0.05
Metal working machinery	73	20 186	123	0.61	4 480	32	0.71	955	10	1.09	14 430	77	0.53
Other industrial machinery & parts	74	92 100	648	0.70	20 925	370	1.77	3 656	47	1.29	65 057	201	0.31
Office machines & ADP equipment	75	120 108	568	0.47	36 520	314	0.86	5 715	56	0.98	74 792	191	0.26
Telecom. & sound recording apparatus	76	76 220	3 094	4.06	27 177	1 664	6.12	3 187	189	5.92	44 152	1 178	2.67
Electrical machinery, apparatus & appliances, n.e.s.	77	143 742	1 907	1.33	45 124	1 003	2.22	8 677	272	3.14	87 540	566	0.65
Road vehicles	78	264 126	370	0.14	95 854	130	0.14	6 690	18	0.27	157 478	205	0.13
Other transport equipment	79	65 703	63	0.10	11 175	27	0.24	3 794	6	0.17	47 323	28	0.06
Miscellaneous manufactures articles	8	373 440	30 078	8.05	101 639	13 936	13.71	28 257	4 616	16.33	236 757	10 677	4.51
Prefabricated buildings, sanitary, heating & lighting fixtures	81	9 913	351	3.54	1 744	199	11.40	305	10	3.26	7 721	128	1.66
Furniture & parts thereof	82	27 924	590	2.11	6 511	274	4.21	1 607	98	6.08	19 532	191	0.98
Travel goods, handbags, etc.	83	8 316	2 384	28.67	2 733	1 078	39.44	1 488	208	14.02	3 903	1 015	26.00
Articles of apparel & clothing accessories	84	109 218	12 928	11.84	29 908	4 447	14.87	9 369	3 252	34.71	68 953	4 814	6.98
Footwear	85	28 855	3 867	13.40	10 732	2 779	25.90	1 636	313	19.15	16 127	683	4.24
Profes. & scientific instruments, n.e.s.	87	43 081	240	0.56	9 264	111	1.20	3 417	18	0.53	29 263	107	0.37
Photo apparatus, optical goods, watches & clocks	88	31 778	764	2.40	8 802	311	3.54	2 538	84	3.29	15 703	358	1.81
Miscellaneous manufactured articles, n.e.s.	89	114 355	8 954	7.83	31 947	4 736	14.83	7 871	632	8.03	77 554	3 381	4.72

Source: OECD, *Foreign Trade by Commodities.*

103

Chapter 4

Policy Conclusions and Implications

Developments since late 1978 provide a wealth of information concerning the role of the opening-up policy in China's transition to a market economy. They cover the reform of the foreign-trade and exchange regimes, the establishment of a legal and institutional framework for foreign direct investment (FDI), and the creation of Special Economic Zones (SEZs) and other development areas. The data supports the claim that these open-economy reforms have been successful in causing strong supply responses to market incentives created by China's opening to the outside world. This experience contrasts sharply with that of eastern Europe and the former Soviet Union, where the transition was accompanied by a fall in production, a contraction of exports, high rates of inflation and increased unemployment.

What makes China different from other economies in transition? What lessons, if any, can be drawn from the Chinese experience? What are the implications of China's transition for the outside world? What are the future prospects for China's open-economy reforms?

China's "Gradual" Approach to Economic Reform

China's transition to a market economy has been characterised by a "gradual" or "evolutionary" approach to economic reform. Many observers contrast this gradualist strategy with the rapid transition strategy — the "big-bang" approach — adopted in the former Czechoslovakia, in Poland and in Russia[1]. With hindsight, some argue that the gradualist approach is more likely to succeed than brutal change. From the viewpoint of allocative efficiency, it is obviously desirable to move as quickly as possible to a market economy. In reality, however, economic transition is a process of institution building and reform designed to establish an effective system of economic management and resource allocation based on market mechanisms. Such institution building associated with economic reform in formerly Socialist countries will inevitably prolong the process of economic transition[2].

McMillan and Naughton (1993, p. 131) emphasize the advantages of "evolutionary" reform by referring to the work of Lindblom (1959), "The Science of 'Muddling Through'":

> ... incremental policy-making — muddling through — works better than grand planning, because the huge amount of information needed to make a comprehensive policy is never fully available; people can agree about a small policy change even if they disagree about ultimate goals; and a comprehensive policy rests heavily on the theory it is built on.

China's economic reform began without a comprehensive blueprint or timetable. Rather, the Chinese authorities adopted a strategy of "feeling for the stones while crossing the river", which allowed Chinese reformers to make various experiments on a limited scale which, when they were successful, encouraged the government to endorse policy changes. A novel feature of China's "muddling through" in this regard is the creation of the Special Economic Zones (SEZs) in which local authorities and enterprises are allowed to experiment with various capitalist practices that cannot be applied immediately to the hinterland under a Communist-controlled political regime. Gradualism allows reform-minded members of the Chinese Communist Party (CCP) to find a pragmatic solution to the politically sensitive issues that may incite resistance from conservative quarters.

A key aspect of China's reform strategy is to enact politically crucial but unspecific "enabling laws" first, which allow the government to introduce more specific policy measures later, when political and economic conditions are met. A case in point is the role of foreign firms in China's economic development. Thanks to the traditional policy of self-reliance under central planning and suspicious views about foreign firms — which were particularly strong during the Cultural Revolution — China had to establish a legal and institutional framework for foreign direct investment (FDI) from scratch. The first measure taken after 1978, when the political wind shifted with respect to FDI, was the landmark 1979 Joint-Venture Law. This was followed by numerous laws and regulations in various areas of direct relevance to both Chinese and foreign firms, including income tax, profit repatriation, labour management, land use and property rights (see Annex 1).

Nevertheless, the Chinese experience should *not* be construed as confirming the view that the gradual approach is the model to follow for other economies in transition. There is no *a priori* reason to believe that piecemeal and partial reforms taken at successive stages in transition will lead to a successful outcome in the long term. China's open-economy reforms and transition experiences simply demonstrate that, though there are different ways of carrying out an economic transition, firm political support and policy continuity is always required. Differences in "initial conditions" amongst economies in transition are of crucial importance for designing and implementing economic reform.

Unlike other transition economies in eastern Europe and the former USSR, the Chinese economy was not in deep macroeconomic crisis prior to the 1978 reforms. The "sense of urgency", which drove some Chinese leaders, notably Deng Xiaoping, to economic reform, came from the recognition that China had failed to realise its development potential because of its "closed-door" policy, and lagged far behind its East Asian neighbours in economic and technological development as a result. This recognition was instrumental in formulating the open-economy reforms. The collapse of Communism in eastern Europe and the former USSR also confirmed the point that "opening up" was the price to be paid for the continued legitimacy of the Chinese Communist Party.

China's Foreign Trade and Investment Regimes

Although the Chinese economy was never completely closed even before the 1978 reforms, foreign trade was controlled rigidly by the central government on the basis of national plans. Actual trade activities were handled by a small number of state-owned foreign trade corporations (FTCs). Trade was simply seen as a balancing item to offset supply-demand gaps under national plans, so that price mechanisms played virtually no role in foreign trade.

In a narrow sense, the process of opening an economy implies a shift in the trade-policy framework through which foreign influences are passed on to the domestic economy. However, in order to take full advantage of economic opportunities provided by direct access to the world market, the opening-up process inevitably requires changes in the overall economic management system, including the reform of policies and institutions that are related to virtually every aspect of economic decision making in a market-economy environment. This involves, *inter alia*, ownership and management reforms, the establishment of markets for goods, services and factors of production, price reforms and economic decentralisation. The initial focus of China's economic reform was on *internal* development, with emphasis on the development of import-substituting industries and the agricultural sector which in the late 1970s employed about 70 per cent of China's total labour force. The exchange rate was also greatly overvalued. Although the ban on foreign direct investment (FDI) was lifted in 1979, the Chinese authorities remained cautious towards FDI. Consequently, China's foreign-trade and investment regimes were strongly inward-oriented at the inception of economic reform.

The conceptual distinction between inward and outward orientation in a country's trade regime is helpful for a better understanding of the evolution of China's open-economy reforms and a major shift in trade regime. An inward-oriented trade regime is generally defined as one favouring production for domestic over export markets by means of high levels of protection, heavy reliance on direct import controls and an overvalued exchange rate. An outward-oriented trade regime, in its broadest sense, is one providing at least as much assistance for export production as for import substitution. Various forms of government intervention, such as incentives for exports, are often used to counterbalance the "anti-export bias" caused by the combination of high import barriers and overvalued exchange rates[3].

In reality, the degree of outward orientation differs widely from country to country and period to period[4]. It is not easy to tell where China's trade regime stands in terms of trade orientation and the degree of protection, partly because of the lack of transparency in trade and other regulations, and because of wide regional differences. It is safe to say, however, that it was in the mid-1980s that the Chinese authorities sent clear signals both at home and abroad that they were intending to establish a trade regime in favour of export production. This period corresponds to

China's *de facto* adoption of the coastal development strategy, an active encouragement of FDI inflows through preferential treatment, and the beginning of successive real effective devaluations of the Chinese yuan.

China's "Export-Push" Strategy

Outward orientation is a common key characteristic of successful countries in East and Southeast Asia. A World Bank study adds further strength to this argument, though there is admittedly "no single East Asian model" (World Bank, 1993c). China's trade pattern during the post-reform period, particularly since the mid-1980s, may be seen as one of these East Asian success stories based on outward orientation, and more precisely, an "export-push" strategy[5].

The logic of an outward-oriented policy is that the adoption of "export promotion" as the primary development objective provides a more rigorous obligation than an inward-oriented policy for policy makers in developing countries to look for the exact policy mix that works and discard what is not working. The combination of fiscal discipline, conservative monetary policy and realistic exchange rates — and the resulting low inflation — is necessary to sustain export growth. Outward orientation is of course not the only component of a successful development strategy in East Asia. Such a strategy also requires appropriate financial policies and institutions, as well as broad-based human capital development. Tautological as this argument may appear, if the aim of development is catching up in productivity terms with developed countries, it follows that making the ability to survive in developed-country markets the overriding criterion to measure the success of business enterprises should appear as a perfectly logical way to proceed. In this respect, the primary goal of an "export-push" strategy is to "increase the market shares of the country's exports in foreign markets" (Bradford, 1993, p. 19). East Asia's single-minded concentration on catching up with a clear-cut target — OECD levels of productivity and per capita income — may be what is unique about its experience. The Socialist ideology forswore using the level of the West as the criterion for development. In spite of the partial nature of its open-economy reforms, China's foreign-trade and investment regimes have provided strong incentives in favour of export promotion as well as protection for import-substituting industries through licensing and other administrative measures.

China's Export Success: Policy Implications for OECD Countries and the Asia-Pacific Region

China has been emerging as a leading Pacific economy in the 1990s and has come to play an important role as a major supplier of manufactured goods to the world market. The country has become the largest non-OECD exporter to the OECD region, and in 1991 became the second largest supplier of manufactured goods, after Taiwan. Thus the implications of China's entry into the world market are of interest to the OECD countries as well as to the developing economies of the Asia-Pacific region.

To assess the relative export performance of China, we used a constant-market-share (CMS) technique with the import data set of the OECD countries with respect to 11 major Asian exporters, compiled from the OECD Commodity Trade Database. The results of the CMS analysis indicate that the rapid increase in manufactured exports from China and Indonesia in 1979-90 and from Thailand in 1985-90 was largely due to a strong competitive effect (Table III-3). This contrasts sharply with the weaker export performances of Hong Kong and Taiwan which were due to a negative or declining competitive effect. These results point to the importance of viewing China's export performance in the context of regional development in Asia and the Pacific. It is inconceivable that the Asian shares of the OECD countries' market could increase *ad infinitum*, since China and its neighbouring developing economies have basically similar export profiles, and are competing with each other for market shares of similar products. China's opening to the outside world can nonetheless be seen as a "positive sum" game, because it provides market opportunities for established exporters in OECD countries as well as in the developing economies of the Asia-Pacific region.

China's coastal development strategy has led to the emergence of a "greater China", comprising the People's Republic of China, Hong Kong and Taiwan. This has been facilitated by industrial restructuring by Hong Kong and Taiwan, which have responded to strong pressures for adjustment arising from both internal and external factors. Growing economic relations between China and Taiwan via Hong Kong since the mid-1980s can be understood as components of the "catching-up" process, described by some trade economists as the "flying-geese" pattern of trade development. The recent development of Taiwanese FDI in China and "two-way" indirect trade across the Taiwan Strait supports this view.

It is reasonable to raise the question of where these "Asian geese" are heading and whether the "flying-geese" pattern of trade development will be sustainable in the 1990s. While various scenarios of future prospects for the Asia-Pacific region are possible, it appears that this specific pattern of trade development amongst the region's developing economies will not be sustainable without large open markets both outside and within the region. Given the strong protectionist sentiment prevailing in some OECD countries, particularly in Europe, it is important for the OECD countries to take a balanced view of China's export growth and its significance for the economic development of both the Asia-Pacific region and the world economy as a whole. It appears that fear of China's rapid growth arises from its sheer size, promoting an assumption that China's exports might soon gobble up the OECD countries' markets. However, this supposition tends to overestimate the dislocations in the OECD countries' economies that could be caused by China's exports, while at the same time underestimating the impact of increased import demand in China on the regional and world economies. Thus, if the development of China — and its neighbouring economies — is to be sustainable, it is crucial that the OECD countries keep their markets open.

Another question concerns the extent to which industry can be transferred from the more advanced Asian economies to China and other developing countries of the region. Due to a heavy dependence on imported inputs for export production, the value-added component of manufactured exports from foreign affiliates in China tends to be very low. The net effect of FDI on the balance of payments could turn out to be negative if the outflow of investment income and royalty payments are taken into account. Furthermore, transfer of technology in human capital-intensive or technology-intensive industries may be very limited; not generally subject to international competition, these sectors have little incentive to adopt the international best practice in production technology.

China has without doubt made a great effort to attract FDI by setting up an appropriate legal framework, creating numerous development zones, lifting restrictions on foreign equity participation, providing tax and other incentives, reforming foreign-exchange and trade regimes, improving industrial infrastructure, liberalising land-leasing, and reducing administrative obstacles. While China's FDI policies may have affected the sectoral and regional distribution of FDI inflows, the trend and pattern of FDI in China has been significantly influenced by macroeconomic factors as well. However, decisions by foreign investors to invest in China do not necessarily depend on whether they are granted special incentives; many developing countries in the Asia-Pacific region provide similar incentives to attract FDI. A side effect of this situation is that the complex system of incentive measures which favour foreign firms over domestic ones promotes rent-seeking activities and leads to misallocation of resources.

China's Open-Economy Reforms: Future Agenda

In spite of the great effort made so far, a long list of policy reforms will still be necessary to sustain the opening-up process. These include:
- the extension of direct trading rights to all enterprises;
- currency convertibility, if only for the current account;
- continued import liberalisation;
- development of open and competitive markets in intermediate and capital goods and factors of production;
- the establishment of transparent and automatic regulations for foreign direct investment, and
- the removal of discriminatory policies in favour of investment in SEZs and other zones.

The above agenda might be expected to remove a good deal of the distortion that is a source of monopoly rents and corruption. During the process of economic transition, China has established markets for goods in which prices are determined by participants in the exchange process. Access to these markets is still limited, however, and there are no clear rules and regulations to prevent the abuse of market power. Thus the markets that exist in China create rents for those with privileged access to them, and people with good *guanxi* (connections) can ensure that the rents accrue to themselves. This limits the overall benefit to be gained from an open economy.

Policy reform in China is a continuing process, however. The Third Plenary Session of the 14th Central Committee of the Communist Party of China, held in November 1993, set the objective of establishing a socialist market economy in China in the coming years. The decision by the Central Committee on 14 November 1993 states that "the establishment of this 'socialist market economic' structure aims at enabling the market to play the fundamental role in resource allocation under macroeconomic control by the State" (*China Daily, Supplement,* 17 November 1993).

The adoption of the five main planks of that objective would imply the continuation and extension of the opening-up process and go some way toward the fulfilment of the agenda set out above. One of the planks in the platform of the socialist market economy is the establishment of "a nationwide integrated and open market system to combine closely the urban market with the rural market and link the domestic market with the international market, so as to optimise the allocation of resources" (*China Daily, Supplement,* 17 November 1993)[6]. The Central Committee decision also points to a "multi-directional opening" of the Chinese economy and further reform of the foreign trade and investment regimes.

The adoption of the objective of a socialist market economy was quickly followed by a series of new policy reforms at the beginning of 1994. These reforms were substantial and included major reforms of the fiscal system, the currency and foreign-exchange system and the trade-policy framework — extending the overall opening up of the economy.

Even the partial removal of barriers to foreign trade and investment have had dramatic effects on the Chinese economy. The most recent reforms indicate that China continues to be committed to the "long march" towards an open-market economy. There is, however, a long way to go — especially in the regulation of markets in order to deal with the growing social division between those with privileged access to markets and those without such access.

Notes and References

1. For a comparative analysis of the two types of economic transition, see Adams (1994), Fischer (1993), Gelb, Jefferson and Singh (1993), McMillan and Naughton (1993), Perkins (1992), and Rana and Dowling (1993).

2. A notable exception is the case of German unification in which the institutions of the Federal Republic of Germany replaced those of the German Democratic Republic.

3. See, for example, Edwards (1993) for an excellent discussion on trade orientation, trade policy reform and economic growth.

4. The World Bank (1987) classified 41 developing economies into four categories by trade orientation: "strongly outward-oriented", "moderately outward-oriented", "moderately inward-oriented" and "strongly inward-oriented" (pp. 82-83). This categorisation is based on four indicators: effective rate of protection, use of direct controls such as quotas and import licenses, use of export incentives and degree of exchange-rate overvaluation. According to these criteria, amongst Asian economies, Hong Kong, Korea and Singapore were classified as "strongly outward-oriented" and Malaysia and Thailand as "moderately outward-oriented" throughout the 1963-85 period. On the other hand, Indonesia, Pakistan, the Philippines and Sri Lanka were classified as "moderately inward-oriented" and Bangladesh and India as "strongly inward-oriented" during the 1973-85 period.

5. See also Bradford (1993) for the "export-push" strategy.

6. The four other planks concern the management mechanism of state-owned enterprises and the establishment of a modern enterprise system; the government's functions in economic management and the establishment of a sound macroeconomic control system; the establishment of an income distribution system; and the establishment of a multilayered social-security system.

Bibliographical References

ADAMS, F.G. (1994), "Economic Transition in China: What Makes China Different?" in LEE, C.H. and H. REISEN (eds), *From Reform to Growth: China and Other Countries in Transition in Asia and Central and Eastern Europe*, OECD Development Centre, Paris.

ANDERSON, K. (1990), *Changing Comparative Advantages in China: Effects on Food, Feed and Fibre Markets*, OECD Development Centre, Paris.

ARIFF, M. and T.E. CHYE (1992), "ASEAN-Pacific Trade Relations", *ASEAN Economic Bulletin*, March, pp. 258-283.

ARMINGTON, P. and U. DADUSH (1993), "The Fourth Growth Pole", *International Economic Insights*, May/June, pp. 2-4.

ASIAN DEVELOPMENT BANK (1993), *Asian Development Outlook 1993*, Oxford University Press, Hong Kong.

BALDINGER, P. (1992), "The Birth of Greater China", *The China Business Review*, May-June, pp. 13-17.

BELL, M. and K. KOCHHAR (1992), "China: An Evolving Market Economy – A Review of Reform Experience", *IMF Working Paper* (WP/92/89), International Monetary Fund, Washington, D.C., November.

BELL, M. *et al.* (1993), "China at the Threshold of a Market Economy", *Occasional Paper*, No. 107, International Monetary Fund, Washington, D.C., September.

BLEJER, M. *et al.* (1991), "China: Economic Reform and Macroeconomic Management", Occasional Paper, No. 76, International Monetary Fund, Washington,D.C., January.

BOHNET, A., Z. HONG and F. MULLER (1993), "China's Open-Door Policy and its Significance for Transformation of the Economic System", *Intereconomics*, July/August, pp. 191-197.

BRADFORD, Jr., C.I. (1993), *From Trade-driven Growth to Growth-driven Trade: Reappraising the East Asian Development Experience*, OECD Development Centre Documents, OECD, Paris.

CHAI, J.C.H. (1989), "Is China Becoming a Leading Pacific Economy?" in CASSEL, D. and G. HEIDUK (eds), *China's Contemporary Economic Reforms as a Development Strategy*, Proceedings of an International Symposium held at the University of Duisburg, June 1989 (pp. 145-163).

CHEN, E.K.Y. (1990), "Economic Outlook for Hong Kong in a Rapidly Changing International Economic Environment", Paper prepared for Tokyo Club Foundation, March.

CHEN, J. (1993), "Social Cost-Benefit Analysis of China's Shenzhen Special Economic Zone", *Development Policy Review*, Vol. 11, No. 3, September, pp. 261-270.

CHIU, L.C. and C. CHUNG (1992), "An Assessment of Taiwan's Indirect Investment Toward Mainland China", *Occasional Paper*, No. 9201, Chung-Hua Institution for Economic Research, Taipei.

CHUNG, C. (1992), "Impacts on Domestic and Host Economies of Taiwan's DFI toward Mainland China", *Occasional Paper*, No. 9202, Chung-Hua Institution for Economic Research, Taipei.

COWLEY, A. (1991), "Survey: Asia's Emerging Economies", *The Economist*, 16 November, pp. 5-24.

CRANE, T.G. (1990), *The Political Economy of China's Special Economic Zones*, London, M.E. Sharpe Inc.

EDWARDS, S. (1993), "Openness, Trade Liberalisation, and Growth in Developing Countries", *Journal of Economic Literature*, Vol. 31, September, pp. 1358-1393.

FINGER, K.M. (1992), "China", (mimeo.) GATT, Geneva, April.

FISCHER, S. (1993), "Socialist Economy Reform: Lessons of the First Three Years", *American Economic Review*, Vol. 83, No. 2, pp. 390-395.

FUKASAKU, K. (1992a), "Economic Regionalisation and Intra-Industry Trade: Pacific Asian Perspectives", *Technical Paper*, No. 53, OECD Development Centre, Paris, February.

FUKASAKU, K. (1992b), "Manufactured Exports and Foreign Direct Investment in China", Paper presented at the Fudan/Sussex University Workshop on *China's Coastal Development Strategy and Pudong New Area*, in Shanghai, 23-25 September.

FUKASAKU, K., C. LEE and D. O'CONNOR (1993), "Trade Policy Profiles of the DAEs", in OECD (1993), *Economic Integration: OECD Economies, Dynamic Asian Economies and Central and Eastern European Countries*, Paris, pp. 37-53.

FUKASAKU, K. and M. WU (1993), "China as a Leading Pacific Economy", *Technical Paper*, No. 89, OECD Development Centre, Paris, November.

FUNKE, N. (1993), "Timing and Sequencing of Reforms: Competing Views and the Role of Credibility", *KYKLOS*, Vol. 46, pp. 337-362.

GARNAUT, R. and G. LIU (eds.) (1992), *Economic Reform and Internationalisation: China and the Pacific Region*, Allen & Unwin, Singapore.

GELB, A., G. JEFFERSON and I. SINGH (1993), "Can Communist Economies Transform Incrementally?: China's Experience", *Policy Research Working Paper*, No. 1189, The World Bank, Washington, D.C.

HARDING, H. (1992), "The US and Greater China", *The China Business Review*, May-June, pp. 18-22.

HARROLD, P. (1992), "China's Reform Experience to Date", *World Bank Discussion Paper* No. 180, Washington, D.C., September.

HARROLD, P. and R. LALL (1993), "China: Reform and Development in 1992-93", *World Bank Discussion Paper*, No. 215, Washington, D.C., August.

HARTLAND-THUNBERG, P. (1990), *China, Hong Kong, Taiwan and the World Trading System*, Macmillan, Hampshire.

HILL, H. and P. PHILLIPS (1993), "Trade is a Two-Way Exchange: Rising Import Penetration in East Asia's Export Economies", *The World Economy*, Vol. 16, No. 6, November, pp. 687-697.

HOWE, C. (1990), "China, Japan and Economic Interdependence in the Asia-Pacific Region", *The China Quarterly*, Vol. 124, December, pp. 662-693.

HSIAO, H.M. and A.Y. SO (1992), "Taiwan-Mainland Economic Nexus: Socio-Political Origins, State-Society Impacts, and Future Prospects", Paper prepared for Workshop on *Investment in Mainland China from East Asia*, East-West Center, Honolulu, May.

HUAN, G-L. (1993), *Foreign Direct Investment and Technology Transfer in China*, D.Phil. Thesis, University of Sussex (unpublished).

HUGHES, H. (1991), "The Impact of Economic Policies on Exports", Paper prepared for Workshop on *China's Exports*, Xiamen, 13-14 September.

HUGHES, H. (ed.) (1992), *The Dangers of Export Pessimism: Developing Countries and Industrial Markets*, International Center for Economic Growth, San Francisco.

JIANG, B. (1992), *China's Dual Exchange Rate System*, D.Phil. Thesis, University of Sussex (unpublished).

JONES, R.S., R.E. KING and M. KLEIN (1993), "Economic Integration between Hong Kong, Taiwan and the Coastal Provinces of China", *OECD Economic Studies*, No. 20, Spring, Paris, pp. 115-44.

KHAN, Z.S. (1991), "Patterns of Direct Foreign Investment in China", *World Bank Discussion Paper*, No. 130, Washington, D.C., September.

KHOR, H.E. (1991), "China – Macroeconomic Cycles in the 1980s", *IMF Working Paper* (WP/91/85), International Monetary Fund, Washington,D.C., September.

KLEINBERG, R. (1990), *China's 'Opening' to the Outside World*, Westview Press, Inc., Boulder, Colorado.

LARDY, N.R. (1992), *Foreign Trade and Economic Reform in China, 1978-1990*, Cambridge University Press, Cambridge.

LARDY, N.R. (1993), "China as a NIC", *International Economic Insights*, May/June, pp. 5-7.

LEAMER, E. AND R. STERN (1970), *Quantitative International Economics* (Chapter 7), Allyn and Bacon, Boston.

LEE, C.H. and H. REISEN (eds) (1994), *From Reform to Growth: China and Other Countries in Transition in Asia and Central and Eastern Europe*, OECD Development Centre, Paris.

LI, W. (1992), "An Analysis On Taiwanese Investment in the Mainland" Paper prepared for Workshop on *Investment in Mainland China from East Asia*, East-West Center, Honolulu, May.

LIN, S. (1991), *Application of Cost-Benefit Analysis in China: A Case Study of the Xiamen Special Economic Zone*, Ph.D. Thesis, Australian National University (unpublished).

LINDBLOM, C.E. (1959), "The Science of 'Muddling Through'", *Public Administration Review*, Vol. 19, pp. 79-88

McMILLAN, J. and B. NAUGHTON (1993), "How to Reform a Planned Economy: Lessons from China", *Oxford Review of Economic Policy*, Vol. 8, No. 1, pp. 130-143.

MOFERT (1992), *Almanac of China's Foreign Economic Relations and Trade 1991/1992*, Beijing.

OBORNE, M.W. (1986), *China's Special Economic Zones*, OECD Development Centre, Paris.

OECD (1993), *Economic Integration: OECD Economies, Dynamic Asian Economies and Central and Eastern European Countries*, Paris.

OZAWA, T. (1990), "Multinational Corporations and the 'Flying-Geese' Paradigm of Economic Development in the Asian Pacific", Paper presented at the 20th Anniversary World Conference on *Multinational Enterprises and 21st Century Scenarios*, in Tokyo, 4-6 July 1990.

PANAGARIYA, A. (1993), "Unravelling the Mysteries of China's Foreign Trade Regime", *The World Economy*, Vol. 16, No. 1, January, pp. 51-68

PERKINS, D.H. (1992), "China's 'Gradual' Approach to Market Reforms", Paper prepared for Conference on *Comparative Experiences of Economic Reform and Post-Socialist Transformation*, 6-8 July 1992, Madrid.

POMFRET, R. (1991), *Investing in China: Ten Years of the Open Door Policy*, Iowa State University Press, Ames.

POMFRET, R. (1992), "Taiwanese Economic Involvement in Jiangsu Province - Some Evidence From Joint Venture Case Studies", Paper prepared for Workshop on *Investment in Mainland China from East Asia*, East-West Center, Honolulu, May.

RANA, P.B. and J.M. DOWLING, JR. (1993), "Big Bang's Bust", *The International Economy*, September/October, pp. 40-72.

RICHARDSON, J.D. (1971), "Some Sensitivity Tests for a 'Constant-Market-Shares' Analysis of Export Growth", *Review of Economics and Statistics*, Vol. 53, August.

RIEDEL, J. (1991), "Intra-Asian Trade and Foreign Direct Investment", *Asian Development Review*, Vol. 9, No. 1, pp. 111-146.

SPENCE, J. (1990), *The Search for Modern China*, London, Hutchinson.

SUNG, Y-W. (1991), *The China-Hong Kong Connection*, Cambridge University Press, Cambridge.

THOBURN, J.T. *et al.* (1992), "Foreign Investment and Economic Liberalisation in China – A Study of Guangdong Province", in ADHIKARI, R., C. KIRKPATRICK and J. WEISS (eds.), *Industrial and Trade Policy Reform in Developing Countries*, Manchester University Press, Manchester, pp. 213-222.

VOGEL, E.F. (1989), *One Step Ahead in China*, Harvard University Press, Cambridge, Mass.

WALL, D. (1992a), "Special Economic Zones and Industrialisation in China", in ADHAKIRI, R., C. KIRKPATRICK and J. WEISS (eds.), *Industrial and Trade Policy Reform in Developing Countries*, Manchester University Press, Manchester, pp. 198-212.

WALL, D. (1992b), "China's Open-economy Reforms and their Achievements" paper prepared for OECD Development Centre, November 1992 (mimeo).

WALL, D. (1993a), "China's Economic Reform and Opening-Up Process: the Special Economic Zones", *Development Policy Review*, Vol. 11, No. 3, September, pp. 243-260.

WALL, D. (1993b), "China's Special Economic Zones" (mimeo), University of Sussex, Brighton.

WALL, D. and K. FUKASAKU (1994), "China's Open Economy Reforms 1978-1992", in LEE, C.H. and H. REISEN (eds), *From Reform to Growth: China and Other Countries in Transition in Asia and Central and Eastern Europe*, OECD Development Centre Documents, OECD, Paris.

WANG Z.M. (1991), "China's Private Economy: Today and Tomorrow", *Beijing Review*, Vol. 34, No. 51.

WANG Z.Z. (1991), "Foreign Direct Investment in China: Performance in the 1980s and Prospects for the 1990s", Institute of Economics of the Chinese Academy of Social Sciences, Beijing.

WORLD BANK (1987), *World Development Report 1987*, Washington, D.C.

WORLD BANK (1988), *China: External Trade and Capital*, Washington, D.C.

WORLD BANK (1989), *China: Macroeconomic Stability and Industrial Growth Under Decentralized Socialism*, Washington, D.C.

WORLD BANK (1990), *China: Between Plan and Market*, Washington, D.C.

WORLD BANK (1992), *China: Reform and the Role of the Plan in the 1990s*, Washington, D.C.

WORLD BANK (1993a), *China: Foreign Trade Reform; Meeting the Challenge of the 1990s*, Washington, D.C.

WORLD BANK (1993b), *China: Managing Rapid Growth and Transition*, Washington, D.C.

WORLD BANK (1993c), *The East Asian Miracle: Economic Growth and Public Policy*, Oxford University Press, Oxford.

WU, M. (1993), "Foreign Direct Investment in China, 1979-1992", paper prepared for OECD Development Centre, August (mimeo).

YAMAZAWA, I. (1990), "Gearing the Japanese Economy to International Harmony", *The Developing Economies*, Vol. 28, No. 1, March, pp. 3-15.

YAMAZAWA, I., A. HIRATA and K. YOKOTA (1991), "Evolving Patterns of Comparative Advantage in the Pacific Economies", in M. ARIFF (ed.), *The Pacific Economy: Growth and External Stability*, Allen & Unwin, London.

YANG, X.G. (1992), "Foreign Funded Enterprises in China", *Beijing Review*, Vol. 35, No. 5/6.

YEATS, A.J. (1991), "China's Foreign Trade and Comparative Advantage – Prospects, Problems and Policy Implications", *World Bank Discussion Paper*, No. 141, Washington, D.C.

ZHAO, B. (1990), "The Hecksher-Ohlin Theorem and Intermediate Goods – The Chinese Economy, 1970-86", *China Working Paper*, No. 90/3, National Centre for Development Studies, Australian National University, Canberra.

ZWEIG, D. (1991), "Internationalizing China's Countryside: The Political Economy of Exports from Rural Industry", *The China Quarterly*, Vol. 128, pp. 716-741.

MAIN SALES OUTLETS OF OECD PUBLICATIONS
PRINCIPAUX POINTS DE VENTE DES PUBLICATIONS DE L'OCDE

ARGENTINA – ARGENTINE
Carlos Hirsch S.R.L.
Galería Güemes, Florida 165, 4° Piso
1333 Buenos Aires   Tel. (1) 331.1787 y 331.2391
Telefax: (1) 331.1787

AUSTRALIA – AUSTRALIE
D.A. Information Services
648 Whitehorse Road, P.O.B 163
Mitcham, Victoria 3132   Tel. (03) 873.4411
Telefax: (03) 873.5679

AUSTRIA – AUTRICHE
Gerold & Co.
Graben 31
Wien I   Tel. (0222) 533.50.14

BELGIUM – BELGIQUE
Jean De Lannoy
Avenue du Roi 202
B-1060 Bruxelles   Tel. (02) 538.51.69/538.08.41
Telefax: (02) 538.08.41

CANADA
Renouf Publishing Company Ltd.
1294 Algoma Road
Ottawa, ON K1B 3W8   Tel. (613) 741.4333
Telefax: (613) 741.5439
Stores:
61 Sparks Street
Ottawa, ON K1P 5R1   Tel. (613) 238.8985
211 Yonge Street
Toronto, ON M5B 1M4   Tel. (416) 363.3171
Telefax: (416)363.59.63
Les Éditions La Liberté Inc.
3020 Chemin Sainte-Foy
Sainte-Foy, PQ G1X 3V6   Tel. (418) 658.3763
Telefax: (418) 658.3763

Federal Publications Inc.
165 University Avenue, Suite 701
Toronto, ON M5H 3B8   Tel. (416) 860.1611
Telefax: (416) 860.1608
Les Publications Fédérales
1185 Université
Montréal, QC H3B 3A7   Tel. (514) 954.1633
Telefax : (514) 954.1635

CHINA – CHINE
China National Publications Import
Export Company (CNPIEC)
16 Gongti E. Road, Chaoyang District
P.O. Box 88 or 50
Beijing 100704 PR   Tel. (01) 506.6688
Telefax: (01) 506.3101

DENMARK – DANEMARK
Munksgaard Book and Subscription Service
35, Nørre Søgade, P.O. Box 2148
DK-1016 København K   Tel. (33) 12.85.70
Telefax: (33) 12.93.87

FINLAND – FINLANDE
Akateeminen Kirjakauppa
Keskuskatu 1, P.O. Box 128
00100 Helsinki
Subscription Services/Agence d'abonnements :
P.O. Box 23
00371 Helsinki   Tel. (358 0) 12141
Telefax: (358 0) 121.4450

FRANCE
OECD/OCDE
Mail Orders/Commandes par correspondance:
2, rue André-Pascal
75775 Paris Cedex 16   Tel. (33-1) 45.24.82.00
Telefax: (33-1) 49.10.42.76
Telex: 640048 OCDE

OECD Bookshop/Librairie de l'OCDE :
33, rue Octave-Feuillet
75016 Paris   Tel. (33-1) 45.24.81.67
(33-1) 45.24.81.81
Documentation Française
29, quai Voltaire
75007 Paris   Tel. 40.15.70.00
Gibert Jeune (Droit-Économie)
6, place Saint-Michel
75006 Paris   Tel. 43.25.91.19
Librairie du Commerce International
10, avenue d'Iéna
75016 Paris   Tel. 40.73.34.60
Librairie Dunod
Université Paris-Dauphine
Place du Maréchal de Lattre de Tassigny
75016 Paris   Tel. (1) 44.05.40.13
Librairie Lavoisier
11, rue Lavoisier
75008 Paris   Tel. 42.65.39.95
Librairie L.G.D.J. - Montchrestien
20, rue Soufflot
75005 Paris   Tel. 46.33.89.85
Librairie des Sciences Politiques
30, rue Saint-Guillaume
75007 Paris   Tel. 45.48.36.02
P.U.F.
49, boulevard Saint-Michel
75005 Paris   Tel. 43.25.83.40
Librairie de l'Université
12a, rue Nazareth
13100 Aix-en-Provence   Tel. (16) 42.26.18.08
Documentation Française
165, rue Garibaldi
69003 Lyon   Tel. (16) 78.63.32.23
Librairie Decitre
29, place Bellecour
69002 Lyon   Tel. (16) 72.40.54.54

GERMANY – ALLEMAGNE
OECD Publications and Information Centre
August-Bebel-Allee 6
D-53175 Bonn   Tel. (0228) 959.120
Telefax: (0228) 959.12.17

GREECE – GRÈCE
Librairie Kauffmann
Mavrokordatou 9
106 78 Athens   Tel. (01) 32.55.321
Telefax: (01) 36.33.967

HONG-KONG
Swindon Book Co. Ltd.
13–15 Lock Road
Kowloon, Hong Kong   Tel. 366.80.31
Telefax: 739.49.75

HUNGARY – HONGRIE
Euro Info Service
Margitsziget, Európa Ház
1138 Budapest   Tel. (1) 111.62.16
Telefax : (1) 111.60.61

ICELAND – ISLANDE
Mál Mog Menning
Laugavegi 18, Pósthólf 392
121 Reykjavik   Tel. 162.35.23

INDIA – INDE
Oxford Book and Stationery Co.
Scindia House
New Delhi 110001   Tel.(11) 331.5896/5308
Telefax: (11) 332.5993
17 Park Street
Calcutta 700016   Tel. 240832

INDONESIA – INDONÉSIE
Pdii-Lipi
P.O. Box 269/JKSMG/88
Jakarta 12790   Tel. 583467
Telex: 62 875

ISRAEL
Praedicta
5 Shatner Street
P.O. Box 34030
Jerusalem 91430   Tel. (2) 52.84.90/1/2
Telefax: (2) 52.84.93
R.O.Y.
P.O. Box 13056
Tel Aviv 61130   Tél. (3) 49.61.08
Telefax (3) 544.60.39

ITALY – ITALIE
Libreria Commissionaria Sansoni
Via Duca di Calabria 1/1
50125 Firenze   Tel. (055) 64.54.15
Telefax: (055) 64.12.57
Via Bartolini 29
20155 Milano   Tel. (02) 36.50.83
Editrice e Libreria Herder
Piazza Montecitorio 120
00186 Roma   Tel. 679.46.28
Telefax: 678.47.51
Libreria Hoepli
Via Hoepli 5
20121 Milano   Tel. (02) 86.54.46
Telefax: (02) 805.28.86
Libreria Scientifica
Dott. Lucio de Biasio 'Aeiou'
Via Coronelli, 6
20146 Milano   Tel. (02) 48.95.45.52
Telefax: (02) 48.95.45.48

JAPAN – JAPON
OECD Publications and Information Centre
Landic Akasaka Building
2-3-4 Akasaka, Minato-ku
Tokyo 107   Tel. (81.3) 3586.2016
Telefax: (81.3) 3584.7929

KOREA – CORÉE
Kyobo Book Centre Co. Ltd.
P.O. Box 1658, Kwang Hwa Moon
Seoul   Tel. 730.78.91
Telefax: 735.00.30

MALAYSIA – MALAISIE
Co-operative Bookshop Ltd.
University of Malaya
P.O. Box 1127, Jalan Pantai Baru
59700 Kuala Lumpur
Malaysia   Tel. 756.5000/756.5425
Telefax: 757.3661

MEXICO – MEXIQUE
Revistas y Periodicos Internacionales S.A. de C.V.
Florencia 57 - 1004
Mexico, D.F. 06600   Tel. 207.81.00
Telefax : 208.39.79

NETHERLANDS – PAYS-BAS
SDU Uitgeverij Plantijnstraat
Externe Fondsen
Postbus 20014
2500 EA's-Gravenhage   Tel. (070) 37.89.880
Voor bestellingen: Telefax: (070) 34.75.778

NEW ZEALAND
NOUVELLE-ZÉLANDE
Legislation Services
P.O. Box 12418
Thorndon, Wellington   Tel. (04) 496.5652
Telefax: (04) 496.5698

NORWAY – NORVÈGE
Narvesen Info Center – NIC
Bertrand Narvesens vei 2
P.O. Box 6125 Etterstad
0602 Oslo 6   Tel. (022) 57.33.00
                               Telefax: (022) 68.19.01

PAKISTAN
Mirza Book Agency
65 Shahrah Quaid-E-Azam
Lahore 54000   Tel. (42) 353.601
                               Telefax: (42) 231.730

PHILIPPINE – PHILIPPINES
International Book Center
5th Floor, Filipinas Life Bldg.
Ayala Avenue
Metro Manila   Tel. 81.96.76
                               Telex 23312 RHP PH

PORTUGAL
Livraria Portugal
Rua do Carmo 70-74
Apart. 2681
1200 Lisboa   Tel.: (01) 347.49.82/5
                               Telefax: (01) 347.02.64

SINGAPORE – SINGAPOUR
Gower Asia Pacific Pte Ltd.
Golden Wheel Building
41, Kallang Pudding Road, No. 04-03
Singapore 1334   Tel. 741.5166
                               Telefax: 742.9356

SPAIN – ESPAGNE
Mundi-Prensa Libros S.A.
Castelló 37, Apartado 1223
Madrid 28001   Tel. (91) 431.33.99
                               Telefax: (91) 575.39.98

Libreria Internacional AEDOS
Consejo de Ciento 391
08009 – Barcelona   Tel. (93) 488.30.09
                               Telefax: (93) 487.76.59

Llibreria de la Generalitat
Palau Moja
Rambla dels Estudis, 118
08002 – Barcelona
             (Subscripcions) Tel. (93) 318.80.12
             (Publicacions) Tel. (93) 302.67.23
                               Telefax: (93) 412.18.54

SRI LANKA
Centre for Policy Research
c/o Colombo Agencies Ltd.
No. 300-304, Galle Road
Colombo 3   Tel. (1) 574240, 573551-2
                   Telefax: (1) 575394, 510711

SWEDEN – SUÈDE
Fritzes Information Center
Box 16356
Regeringsgatan 12
106 47 Stockholm   Tel. (08) 690.90.90
                               Telefax: (08) 20.50.21

Subscription Agency/Agence d'abonnements :
Wennergren-Williams Info AB
P.O. Box 1305
171 25 Solna   Tel. (08) 705.97.50
                               Téléfax : (08) 27.00.71

SWITZERLAND – SUISSE
Maditec S.A. (Books and Periodicals - Livres
et périodiques)
Chemin des Palettes 4
Case postale 266
1020 Renens   Tel. (021) 635.08.65
                               Telefax: (021) 635.07.80

Librairie Payot S.A.
4, place Pépinet
CP 3212
1002 Lausanne   Tel. (021) 341.33.48
                               Telefax: (021) 341.33.45

Librairie Unilivres
6, rue de Candolle
1205 Genève   Tel. (022) 320.26.23
                               Telefax: (022) 329.73.18

Subscription Agency/Agence d'abonnements :
Dynapresse Marketing S.A.
38 avenue Vibert
1227 Carouge   Tel.: (022) 308.07.89
                               Telefax : (022) 308.07.99

See also – Voir aussi :
OECD Publications and Information Centre
August-Bebel-Allee 6
D-53175 Bonn (Germany)   Tel. (0228) 959.120
                           Telefax: (0228) 959.12.17

TAIWAN – FORMOSE
Good Faith Worldwide Int'l. Co. Ltd.
9th Floor, No. 118, Sec. 2
Chung Hsiao E. Road
Taipei   Tel. (02) 391.7396/391.7397
                    Telefax: (02) 394.9176

THAILAND – THAÏLANDE
Suksit Siam Co. Ltd.
113, 115 Fuang Nakhon Rd.
Opp. Wat Rajbopith
Bangkok 10200   Tel. (662) 225.9531/2
                               Telefax: (662) 222.5188

TURKEY – TURQUIE
Kültür Yayinlari Is-Türk Ltd. Sti.
Atatürk Bulvari No. 191/Kat 13
Kavaklidere/Ankara   Tel. 428.11.40 Ext. 2458
Dolmabahce Cad. No. 29
Besiktas/Istanbul   Tel. 260.71.88
                               Telex: 43482B

UNITED KINGDOM – ROYAUME-UNI
HMSO
Gen. enquiries   Tel. (071) 873 0011
Postal orders only:
P.O. Box 276, London SW8 5DT
Personal Callers HMSO Bookshop
49 High Holborn, London WC1V 6HB
                               Telefax: (071) 873 8200
Branches at: Belfast, Birmingham, Bristol, Edin-
burgh, Manchester

UNITED STATES – ÉTATS-UNIS
OECD Publications and Information Centre
2001 L Street N.W., Suite 700
Washington, D.C. 20036-4910 Tel. (202) 785.6323
                               Telefax: (202) 785.0350

VENEZUELA
Libreria del Este
Avda F. Miranda 52, Aptdo. 60337
Edificio Galipán
Caracas 106   Tel. 951.1705/951.2307/951.1297
                    Telegram: Libreste Caracas

Subscription to OECD periodicals may also be
placed through main subscription agencies.

Les abonnements aux publications périodiques de
l'OCDE peuvent être souscrits auprès des
principales agences d'abonnement.

Orders and inquiries from countries where Distribu-
tors have not yet been appointed should be sent to:
OECD Publications Service, 2 rue André-Pascal,
75775 Paris Cedex 16, France.

Les commandes provenant de pays où l'OCDE n'a
pas encore désigné de distributeur devraient être
adressées à : OCDE, Service des Publications,
2, rue André-Pascal, 75775 Paris Cedex 16, France.

9-1994

OECD PUBLICATIONS, 2 rue André-Pascal, 75775 PARIS CEDEX 16
PRINTED IN FRANCE
(41 94 13 1) ISBN 92-64-14290-8 - No. 47573 1994